I0829519

ENCHANTING NEELI

First Love. Second Time.

ENCHANTING NEELI

First Love. Second Time.

Sanjeev Kotnala

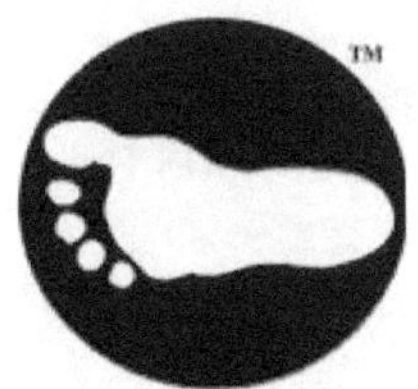

Bigfoot Publications
Because, there's a writer in everyone.

Enchanting Neeli : First love. Second Time
Author : Sanjeev Kotnala

First Published by
Bigfoot06 Publications (OPC) Pvt. Ltd.
1st floor, BSR Building, Near Vishal Mega Mart,
Daultabad Flyover, Laxman Vihar Phase 3,
Gurugram, Haryana (122001)
Website: www.bigfootpublications.in
Email: info@bigfootpublications.in

First Edition : February, 2024
© Sanjeev Kotnala

ISBN Print Book : 9798884585942

All rights reserved. No part of this book may be reproduced or transmitted in any form or by any means, electronic or mechanical, including photocopying, recording, or by an information storage and retrieval system—except by a reviewer who may quote brief passages in a review to be printed in a magazine, newspaper, or on the Web—without permission in writing from the copyright owner.

Although the author and publisher have made every effort to ensure the accuracy and completeness of information contained in this book, we assume no responsibility for errors, inaccuracies, omissions, or any inconsistencies herein. Any slights on people, places, or organizations are unintentional.

Typeset in Palatino Linotype 12pt
by Yachika Prajapati For Bigfoot06 Publications

Printed in India

Dedicated to my Mother

Mrs. Kanchan Lata Kotnala
My Yesterday, Today And Tomorrow.

And to my wife
Neha (Mamta) Kotnala
She is all the encouragement I need.

*This is a work of fiction.
Names, characters, businesses, places, and incidents
are the product of the author's imagination.
Any resemblance to any person, living or dead,
or events is purely coincidental.*

Immortalising Love
A note from the author

Love is an eternal emotion. Surprisingly, most epic love stories end in tragedy. Does that mean that love without pain is inferior? Is separation a vital part of a memorable love story? Hence, a question arises, why do we not hear more about the 'happily ever after' love stories?

The fact remains that millions of love stories take birth every moment, but only a few realise their potential. Most love stories are sacrificed on the altar of societal constraints, norms, unsaid rules, family responsibility and expectations.

Irrespective of how the love story ends, life moves on. Memories fade, and the promises are forgotten. People adopt new life, while the heart bleeds in private. Many times, people end up laughing at their own passion and emotions at a later stage. Society forces everyone to wear a mask of happiness. However, a lucky few end up spending their lives with their love. And a few of them enjoy lifelong togetherness. Some lucky ones do get more than a chance.

'Enchanting Neeli' takes inspiration from other love stories I have heard or read. I may have stolen a few moments from them and topped it with my imagination to make a heady mocktail. Don't blame me if you see a reflection of yourself in it.

Hope you enjoy this simmering mocktail of a love story.

Come join me in the land of dreams, take a ringside seat and get a perfect view of the life of Rahul.

Sanjeev Kotnala

TABLE OF CONTENTS

PART- I
TODAY - THE TRAP

Beautiful Day

Rahul plays with her long silky hair. They are soft. He likes it when she keeps her hair open. He knows her red hairband is somewhere in the room, and later they will end up searching for it. They have spent the last few hours making love. He feels her body eagerly pushing against his, and she wants him to hold her tight. He obliges. Surprisingly, he is still trying to remember her name. He touches her firm breast and continues to play with her erect nipples. She responds, cuddling into him. Her face still buried in his hairy chest. He tenderly lifts her face, and then it hits him; he knows the face. He has seen it before. She slowly opens her eyes, and he tries to see into them. He knows she should not have been with him.

***

Rahul, the practical optimist, wakes up to yet another beautiful day. He firmly believes in the duality in life. There is happiness and sadness. Every day is the same, and what matters is what you make of it. Every day is a string of mini-episodes loudly screaming for continuity and attention.

Like any other day in life, today is yet another opportunity to write a fresh chapter in the story called life. In Rahul's case, life behaves like a biased casino table. Maybe only Rahul sees it this way because he over-analyses every episode, character and relationship. He seeks logic and relevance where none needs to exist.

If you were to see life from Rahul's point of view, it is an elaborate saga of misguided adventures.

Life is nothing but a series of purposeful transactions. There is a purpose in everything. It is different; one may not be aware of it, fail to recognise it, or just don't acknowledge it. There are different perspectives on the same thing, and it is confusing. Rahul has often tried seeing things from another person's perspective, but it never helped the cause. He knows that getting into another person's shoes is easy to say but tough to do. And finally, what matters is how you see the situation.

Today is no different. Sun has taken its own sweet time to casually leapfrog the tall building on the eastern side and then announced itself with loud friendly sunbeams entering his room. However, this sweeping energy does not help him wipe the anxiety gripping him. The feeling is not new for him. He is anxious because he thinks, and he thinks because he always wants to be in control.

Rahul has been waiting for this day.

Today, if his plans work, things may change in his life. He knows it is foolish to enter the ocean of chaotic emotions and expect calmness. life is so unpredictable, and there is no surety. And he, like a gambler, must place his bets.

Things change, and they must with time. You never know if you will win or lose, and the only thing in your control is the bets you place. You can only win a jackpot if you buy the ticket. It is this simple.

Today, he is going all-in, playing the biggest gamble of his life.

***

December 2011. It is foggy in Delhi. It is neither cold enough to freeze nor warm enough to step out without woollens. *Delhiwaali Gulabi thand*[1]. It is around 7 degrees outside and predicted to touch a comfortable 15 degrees during the day, making it a sunny day compared to the bone-chilling cold of the last week.

Everyone needs something to hold to life. Rahul lives life on his terms, and he has finally found something he would like to hold on to for the rest of his life.

Today, the rejuvenated and re-energised Rahul's mantra will be tested. 'People who matter don't mind, and people who mind don't matter.'

***

It is six in the morning, and Delhi wears a deserted look. Only the hard-wired walkers dare to step out before 8 a.m. Most walkers wait for the sun to come out and the fog to thin down before they get out of their comfort zone. And on most of the days, they are late for their walk.

---

[1] The early period of cold months - when the initial cold gives a pleasing feeling.

It is Sunday, and Rahul is in no hurry.

Delhi and *Delhiwalaa's*[2] slowdown in winter. But Rahul refuses to waste time cuddled inside a warm *Rajai*[3] sipping hot chai. He is up and out on his morning walk. It is his escape from otherwise a reasonably disciplined and organised life and today a part of his well-thought-out plan.

It's been a few years since Rahul retired from Government services at the ripe age of 60. It is a different thing that he considers himself to be young. Make that - young at heart. He carries the sprinkled silvery-white hair as a sign of pride and experience. He smiles when people compliment his looks, telling him he does not look the age.

***

Rahul continues jogging in Lodhi Gardens, situated behind the India International Centre. The Ninety acres of Lodhi garden is sandwiched between Khan Market on one side and Safdarjung's Tomb on the other, a mere three kilometres from another neglected monument; Humayun's Tomb.

The tomb of Sayyid and the Lodhi rulers of the 15th century is another well-known attraction of the Lodhi garden. The not-so-green overused jogging track at the garden encircles Bara Gumbad[4], a three-domed mosque and Sheesh Gumbad.

---

[2] Residents of Delhi.
[3] Quilt.
[4] Dome.

Most joggers start with a clear understanding of the number of rounds they plan to run. Rahul finds it funny to have targets for such simple activities in life. He runs or jogs because he wants to and stops when he feels tired or no longer wishes to run.

Why complicate life? There are better things to worry about.

Rahul's earlier approach to exercising was *'Kal Se... Kal Se[5],'* until he met Dr Wadhera at Sir Ganga Ram hospital, who gave him an ultimatum. Rahul joked, "Why are you getting so serious? It is just a few parameters acting naughty in the check-up".

Dr Wadhera gave Rahul the option of a lifelong medication or doing something about the rising cholesterol level and the near diabetic readings. Rahul picked the latter.

Jogging was his idea of an escape and to start the day on a good note.

Every morning Rahul leaves home to jog for a minimum of 30 minutes. He diligently follows it till his young-in-mind body refuses to take any more strain. Jogging has helped Rahul. His knees no longer groan when he gets up in the morning, and he is a bit slimmer at the waist.

At Lodhi Garden, Rahul tries to keep pace with the youngsters, but they leave him far behind. He puts

---

[5] A way of saying will do it from tomorrow, a promise from tomorrow-a tomorrow that never comes.

everything into his run and smiles when he sees some ladies watching him, and there is pride in his smile.

At the far end, near the Sheesh Gumbad, Rahul tries not to be judgmental about the Laughter Club members. He kicks in with the last burst of energy, managing to pass a few of the youngsters. They hate it and soon return the favour. Rahul lacks the motivation to push himself and break their bubble of happiness. He knows he will fail in his efforts and thinks it is worthless at his age to attempt. Rahul allows the young brigade to outrun a person twice their age and feel better. He smiles. That was his one good deed for the day.

***

After retirement, Rahul is in total control of his time or so he wants to believe. He has more time on hand despite doing too many new things, and his perfectionist approach stops him from cutting corners.

Writing his debut novel is at the top of his to-do list. Honestly, he has not done much about it, and even the interest shown by one of the Daryaganj[6] publishers has not been enough to push him. He knows writing his own story *Aap Beethi*[7], will be emotionally draining and thus has been delaying the inevitable.

He knows, with his story, he risks upsetting a few people. It is a good story. It may even interest curious

---

[6] A place/street in Delhi near LalQuilla (Red Fort) where most publishers have offices and shops.
[7] Self-experienced

millennials and maybe work as an OTT series. However, some characters are still alive. And it will be tough to camouflage their identities. Rahul does not want to be sued for sharing the truth.

The other problem is the story itself.

The story has too many subplots, and his rich imagination has corrupted the storyline. He needs to rework and find the right balance between reality, fiction and fantasy.

To get the story right and at least to lay the foundation for a detailed script, Rahul enrolled in the 'Writer Training Workshop' at the British Library. He even once enquired about the Himalayan Writer's Retreat in Uttarakhand. But, then, he is the classical Kal se-Kal se-type of person.

Now, looking back at his adult life, Rahul can see it from a different perspective. He wants to write the story. And sometime in future, he promises to write the story. Maybe the laughter club too will make a guest appearance in it.

The unnecessary anxiety and increasing number of questions are essential to Rahul's life.

Rahul has learnt to move with the flow of the turbulent river called life by taking the path of least resistance. Breaking banks whenever the flow of emotions crossed his limited threshold. The river of Rahul's life, an epitome of uncontrollable fury, is full of undercurrents with many rapids to negotiate.

Maybe that is how stories develop in the whirlpool of life and later find the audience they deserve. Perhaps his story, too, will morph with time and the shifting perspectives of the readers. He knows it is a story that the audience would hate or love. It is, after all, a part of his life.

Song of Life

Rahul readjusts the wires of his iPod. There is no music flowing through them; they are his excuse from unwarranted socialising. He hates exchanging fake pleasantries with people beyond his close circle. Thanks to the earphones, not only is he spared of such interactions, but he is also free to observe people.

The only music Rahul hears while jogging is himself silently humming his favourite song. The song is loud and clear in his head. It always comes in bits and pieces with a tune of its own. Humming the song for Rahul is an intensely personal experience and mystical to some extent.

Rahul needs no appreciation for his singing capabilities. Only he can hear the song, and for him, his singing is always in sync. Rahul is biased, but he is no different than any one of us.

Rahul keeps humming the song. However, he does not notice his somewhat relentless loud humming irritating others. Sometime in the next few hours, he will suddenly stop singing. But then, dreams and fantasies will take over.

Rahul cannot stop thinking of his past.

What could have happened if only something else had happened?

How would his life be different?

It is tough not to remember the first love, kiss, look, sex and many other things.

Sometimes you fail your dreams, and sometimes dreams fail you.

Failure is part of life. There is no point in blaming yourself for what happened or did not happen. No one else knows it better than Rahul. He has failed to keep his promises to her, whom he often meets in his dreams.

***

Things have a rhythm to themselves, just like uncontrolled chaos has a rhythm, and most fail to comprehend this simple reality. Rahul's problem is his relentless hope to decode the rhythm and the chaos. He is coiled inside, which is not a new feeling for him.

Suddenly the entire song comes to him. It is the song etched on his subconscious. A song he denies even exists. The song randomly leaps into his consciousness and surfaces on his lips. Getting the tune right, his humming picks up the tempo.

When did the song start? Was it when he saw the couple walking hand in hand? Or did it start when he saw the kids on the swings laughing? Does it matter? All that is relevant is that the song and the singer are there, and they can find their own peace and pace.

Rahul can't control the song. Once he starts humming it, he can do nothing to stop. His head is like an echo chamber, further amplifying the song. Honestly, Rahul has no interest in stopping it, and it gives him peace of a different type which is addictive.

The lyrics are a mystery to him. In the past, he had tried Googling them, but Google Chacha8 failed. So, Rahul is happy humming parts of the lyrics, filling the gaps with some reasonably good substitutes. He hums the freshly rehashed song. It does not matter what the original song was. The meaning and the meter of the song remain unchanged. Or so Rahul would want you to believe and think.

He first heard the song at the *Dasherra*9 celebration a few decades back. There, the cute chubby singer from Shahani Orchestra had the audience spellbound. She called it a song with a soul, the song of complete bliss. It is a song of memories for Rahul, and every word takes him back by 35-37 years.

With the song, the memories flood his mind. The song does not allow Rahul to be himself.

***

The gates of Lodhi Garden look inviting. They urge Rahul to stop and head for the safe sanctuary of home.

---

8 Uncle
9 Indian festival celebrated at the end of 9 days of Navratri. A celebration of Good winning over Evil and Truth over non-truths. It is the day Lord Rama defeated the mighty Ravana.

It is 6:30 a.m. He marks himself for the last round. Maybe the song will fully reveal itself.

Rahul crosses the laughter group. He nods and smiles; a few wave back, acknowledging his existence. He and the group have developed a nameless relationship because they share time and space.

Rahul continues humming. The song breaks open memories, and the lyrics find a smooth flow. Tears, as usual, find their way to the corner of his eyes, and he acknowledges them by carelessly wiping them. Yes, the song has a story to tell.

Sona Na Chandi Na Koi Mahal, Tumko Mai Dey Sakunga,

Magar Tu Karey Eek Vada,Tu Mujhse Mohabbat Karegi,

Sukh Dukh Ka Saathi Banunga, Chota Sa Ghar Eek Mai Dunga[10].

Rahul is fighting an internal battle between emotions and desires. For a long time, he has been working on adding colours of future possibilities and opportunities on the limitless canvas of his life.

During his tenure with the Tourism Department, Rahul and his team often used the term- probortunity[11]. A problem or an opportunity? A problem can be converted into an opportunity, and an opportunity can lead to problems.

---

[10] Translated- I will not provide you with gold or silver or a place/ but if you promise to love me/ I will be always there with you in happiness and sorrow/ I will give you a small home.

[11] Probortunity- The author does not claim to define or create this word, which is now regularly used in management circles.

Rahul believes life is full of probortunities, and it is up to the individual what to make of them. Decide what is important to them and what is not. For most of his life, Rahul failed to be friends with opportunities, but that is Rahul.

Was it destiny that their path crossed? Is it destiny that is again pushing him?

It has been more than 35 years, and he has no answers. Maybe the truth is lost in the archives of time. And maybe truth matters a lot less than what he thinks.

There, now everything is sorted out.

Rahul moved on in life. Maybe the probortunities and the scar, the possibilities scared him. However, this story is not about the scars but the healing.

The Beginning

When alone, Rahul likes to take a trip down memory lane. Thinking of life and possibilities. How different it could have been if only he had acted when the situation demanded his intervention. Rahul knows fantasies have their own place in life, and they are crueller than dreams, and dreams, like realities, are ruthless. The dreams and desires haunt and hurt, but knowing it does not stop Rahul from revisiting episodes of adulthood that could have changed his life.

Rahul leads a simple life but he questions everything. Why did it happen the way it did? Why did life take a turn that Rahul never wanted? Maybe he is the only person who questions God when things go wrong and even when things go right for him. His wise friends have repeatedly told him that time has all the answers and that the wounds would heal with time. Rahul knows it is not true. The wounds may heal, but the pain will remain forever. And maybe it is better that way.

Rahul is seen as a polite person, and behind that politeness is a person full of confidence and determination. He dares to make unpopular decisions and not care. Honestly, he is a survivor in many ways.

Possibilities and temptations have been part of Rahul's life. Despite tempting assignments across the country and a few abroad, Rahul managed to remain unscarred - untainted. He shunned the bold hints of pleasure and sin. His friends laugh and question him. Is it an achievement to stay unscarred when you refuse to play with fire? They fail to see Rahul's perspective.

What Rahul managed is precious. He sleeps peacefully with no worries, and that is what matters to him. He has done well not to have many regrets.

The only thing Rahul misses is his wife, Sanjana.

A few years back, Sanjana left him for an unexplored destination called heaven.

Sanjana never questioned Rahul on matters outside their home. However, she drew the line and took all the calls when it came to their home. The unsaid territories firmed up with time.

Sanjana was the queen of the home, and Rahul was the king of the outside world. Life was simple, with Rahul taking decisions that had anything to do with the world outside. And Sanjana never challenged him, at least not in public.

Sanjana called the shots inside the four walls and in the close family circle. She knew Rahul hated family gatherings and was an unwilling social failure but Sanjana not only dictated but ensured that Rahul attended family functions. However, she could not teach Rahul the art of conversation. And to hide this weakness, Rahul religiously avoided social gatherings and functions where there was a chance to meet close relatives. No socialising meant no need to talk, and that meant no fake pleasantries. It was the way Rahul wanted, and over time, Sanjana became the face of the family at social functions.

Sanjana left Rahul much before Girish, their son, was married into the Jugran family. A family Sanjana liked and approved of. In fact, much before Girish's graduation Sanjana had been busy matchmaking. Whenever Sanjana and Rahul met Mr. & Mrs. Jugran, Sanjana magically steered the conversations to the possibility of Girish marrying their daughter Shilpa.

***

Nowadays, whenever Rahul thinks of Sanjana, another face pops up. A face that only he knows.

Rahul is 60 plus with a grown-up son and a beautiful *sanskari*[12] daughter-in-law. Everyone expects him to think only of Sanjana. Societal expectations prohibit him from acknowledging another woman in his life. However, the face that frequently appears before him is not of Sanjana. It magically makes him think hard, raising more questions than he can answer.

It has been years since he last met the face overpowering his life.

In that sense, nothing much has changed.

---

[12] Cultured or one who follows all the right culture and religious dictates.

Garmiyo Mai Pahado Mai Jakey Pyaar Ki Geet Gaya karengey[13].

***

Rahul's marriage was an arranged marriage. He married Sanjana in October, and they went to Manali for the honeymoon in December! There they stayed at the 'New Snow View Bungalow,' right at the turn for the Rohtang pass. Manali in December was too cold for their comfort. It was freezing. They had a lovely view of snow-capped mountains from the room and there was no urge to open the windows.

Other than the customary RohtangPass[14] and a trip to Manikaran for the hot spring and famous Golden grass15, they gave Manali a royal silent ignore.

Rahul hummed the song's next line, which was apt for the situation.

Garm Leehafo Mai Chipkar, Kisseyh Sunaya Karengey[16].

Like most other tourists, Sanjana and Rahul went to Rohtang Pass and enjoyed throwing snowballs at each other. Young at body and heart, they bridged the gap between themselves with every throw until there was

---

[13] Translation- When summers come, we will go to the mountains, and all we will only talk about is love.

[14] Rohtang Pass is a high mountain road (13000 ft) on the eastern Pir Panjal Range of the Himalayas, around 51 km from Manali. It connects the Kullu Valley with the Lahaul and Spiti Valleys of Himachal Pradesh,

[15] Golden Grass comes from the gold-coloured grass. In Manali, it also refers to a speciality weed available at Manikarn. It is supposed to be one of the best grades.

[16] We will hide in the warmth of the quilt and tell each other stories.

no more space separating them. They hugged; it was a natural thing for the newlyweds to do.

There are few things Rahul remembers about the Manali trip other than what they indulged in inside the closed doors. Things like a hot cup of Maggie, customary pictures against snow-capped mountains, visiting a few temples, dipping his fingers in the ice-cold water of river Beas[17] and getting surprised by the resultant numbness. Simple pleasures indeed make for perfect memories.

At the end of the first day, Sanjana and Rahul found better options inside, like exploring each other. It was their first step into a new relationship which needed no definition. They slowly opened up to each other to complete emotional nakedness.

Sanjana's suggestion of 'Total transparency. Hiding nothing' became their philosophy of happy married life. At Manali, they shared everything about their lives, freely allowing the trapped emotions and secrets to surface. They searched and found words and gestures to express the unexpressed. Naturally, it was emotionally draining. At every stage, there was enough unsaid that was never questioned. However, they never thought about how deep to open up.

Happiness, Success, Failure. Love, Hate, Desires, Ambitions, Aspirations and Fantasies were out in the open. Every life episode was shared, punctuated with

---

[17] River Beas starts from a small opening at 14,308 feet on the southern face of Rohtang Pass.

the unsatiated hunger of physical craving ending in the pleasurable act of oneness.

The best part was about sharing their infatuations with the partner's gaze. It was not that tough, as no questions were asked!

Rahul told Sanjana about Anita and his one-sided romance, about Beena, and how she changed his life. Sanjana told him about Abhishekh, her love and past that sometimes bothered her. They emptied their cupboards and were ready for the new life. Even though there were no more secrets and stories to share, they promised to take another vacation soon.

Samundar Kinarey, Seepo Se Moti Chunengey[18]

Goa was the natural choice for the next vacation, but it took them three years. They went to Goa in April, like eager teenagers trying to make up for the lost time. Rahul termed it their second honeymoon. 'Definitely not like the one in Manali,' Sanjana had winked. Rahul heard the inviting naughtiness, and it was all the encouragement he needed.

After a few years, they revisited Goa to welcome their son Girish into the family. Through Girish's eyes, once again, Rahul lived his childhood.

***

Girish was a pampered child. He got whatever he asked for.

---

[18] We will go next to the sea and pick pearls from oysters.

Rahul once bought Girish a soft toy, a teddy bear. Sanjana laughed. 'Hey Rahul, Girish is your son, not your daughter.' Rahul smiled and let her on to a secret he missed sharing at Manali.

Rahul's family was a typical middle-income household with its own challenges. Forget the branded toys; Rahul never had a hand-me-down variety. His toys were home-crafted by his mother, and maybe that's why Rahul's dreams were full of toys. At the top of the list was a big branded teddy bear.

It was all about childhood memories.

There was a girl who lived close by. She had a neat-looking pink teddy bear. Rahul and the girl would play, but the teddy was a complete no-go zone. She never allowed Rahul to touch it. The childhood scars and the craze for a teddy bear never left him. He was a victim of the territorial battle where the advantages came with owning a toy. It irritated him, making him feel inferior. By buying his son a teddy bear, Rahul took a step closer to cleanse his troubled past.

Sanjana hugged him. Softly kissing him on the earlobes. She murmured, 'Oh, my sweet teddy bear,' which led to another round of passionate lovemaking.

Today, when Rahul sees a teddy bear, he no longer feels deprived; childhood scars have somewhat been taken care of. But, he would find ways and means to get whatever Girish asked for; that was not negotiable as far as Rahul was concerned. He did not want Girish to have the semi-deprived childhood he had in Agra.

Girish was excellent in his studies.

Rahul, in his school, was a 'Can do better' type of kid, always getting the 'can do better' remark in the report card. Girish, on the other side, was an 'Excellent' kid, helping improve the family average.

Girish, now 25, did his post-graduation from IIM Ahmedabad and works for a multinational FMCG[19] company based in Delhi. Almost like a family tradition, Girish married early. Shilpa Jugran, his wife, like his mother Sanjana, is a homemaker by choice. Girish believes, whatever he achieved in life, the credit goes to his mother, who was always available to guide him in any situation, to tell him what was wrong and right. Rahul endorses the thought and in turn, gives his mother all the credit for whatever he has achieved.

***

Rahul's job required frequent changes in cities. However, Sanjana remained with the kids, which meant that Sanjana and Rahul lived in different cities for many years. Whenever Rahul tried convincing her to move with him, she would say, 'If our love is real, distances will fan the fire, and if it is not, the distance will anyway kill it. So, why bother.'

Sanjana would playfully question Rahul, if he was not confident to take the test of time and distance? Who was Rahul doubting? She or himself?

---

[19] FMCG Fast-moving consumer goods. Like Oil and soaps.

Rahul had no answers to her questions, so he remained quiet.

He knew some questions were best left unanswered.

***

Shilpa, his daughter-in-law and Girish's wife, constantly reminds Rahul of the face he knows, which was part of his growing years and will always have a special meaning.

If Sanjana was alive, this would have been considered emotional cheating. Rahul still felt he was in some way cheating. But he could not help it. In such moments, Rahul takes a deep breath and repeats the vows he took with Sanjana. Promises that he has managed to keep till she was alive.

Thanks to Manali, there was nothing hidden. Sanjana knew the story and the face, but she was no longer with Rahul.

Roothegi Tu Meri Jaan, Tujhko Manaya Karunga

Huskey Honto Pe Lekhar Tera Naam Pukara Karoonga[20].

---

[20] When you are upset, I will make you happy and will call out your name

Album

6:45 AM, Rahul finally steps out of Lodhi Garden and climbs into his Mitsubishi Lancer. The drive to Defence Colony is a short one. He drives on autopilot, unconsciously reacting to the traffic ahead.

Subconsciously, he is back in Agra.

Teenage memories flood his mind. Especially the one from the best time of his life.

Sona Na Chandi Na Koi Mahal Tujhko Mai Dey Sakunga.

Magar Eek Vada Karunga, Tujhse Mohabbat Mai Karungaa

Sukh Dukh Ka Saathi Banunga, Chota Sa Ghar Mai Dunga

He takes the turn after the flyover. Soon he will be home. Sweet home the place with fond memories of love and occasional fights helping love to survive and flourish. The rare fights made them realise the importance of togetherness and interdependence. Otherwise, in a hectic life, love suffocates under the twin pressures of expectations and experiences. It would have been tough for love to survive.

Rahul parks the car but does not bother to ring the bell. Instead, he uses the open French windows on the ground floor to get in.

Girish, his son, is busy reading the Hindustan Times. Seeing Rahul, Girish gets up and touches his feet. Traditional ritual over, both friendly father-son duo start the morning banter. Rahul is still humming the song.

'WOW, dad, you and singing! What say, getting romantic at this age? Did you finally find someone in the park? Girish tries to lighten the mood.

'Tell me, Pa, and I will invite her for dinner'. Shilpa joins in the conversation and, as usual, starts making plans.

Shilpa is the pivot around whom the family moves. She is like a daughter to Rahul. A daughter he never had.

'Sanjana, see, the kids are trying to get me to get married again' Rahul looks up at Sanjana's framed picture in her bridal attire and humorously complains.

Many years back, even before the arrival of Girish, Rahul had promised Sanjana that the only picture of her he would ever share publicly would be in the bridal dress. That is how he wants everyone to see and remember his Sanjana.

All other pictures of Sanjana are safely locked in a small black suitcase.

Sometimes in the late evenings, Rahul sits alone and sees the pictures while slowly sipping his favourite whisky, reviving old memories of the time Sanjana and he spent together.

Rahul continues, 'Girish, it's hardly been five years since your mother left us.' He immediately realises time had nothing to do with the situation and the comment. And just then, the other face floats in his vision. Someone else is dominating Rahul's mind.

'So what, Dad, Maa will never mind; you were a perfect husband. Dad, I know her, and she will want you to be always happy and singing like today'.

Girish looks at the picture of his mother and mockingly asks, 'What, Mom, you agree *na*[21].'

'Who said I am not happy.'

'So, there is no one, Dad.'

'NO'

'Okay, don't get angry, Pa, remember shouting is not good for your blood pressure', Shilpa patronises her father-in-law and brings Rahul's medicines and a glass of cold milk. She places them on the study table next to the Green Album, which Rahul has strategically placed before going for his morning walk.

The Green Album is full of beautiful memories. Stories trapped in old pictures hide multiple emotions in every frame, still telling only a part of the story. Only the people in the frame know the moment and actual incident.

---

[21] Na in Hindi means NO. However, when spoken this way, it almost means you agree with me.

Rahul had strategically placed the album before going for his walk. However, he has not got the desired reaction from Girish or Shilpa. Seems like the bait has failed, and he will have to take the lead.

"Where did you get this album from,' Rahul looks at Girish.

'Oh, Dad, don't know, it was here only. Shilpa and I were going through the pictures. Nice old black and white pictures. Did you guys not have candid pictures at that time, everywhere everyone was posing.'

'Oh.' Rahul fakes disinterest.

'And dad, only you could keep them like this. Every picture has a date & year mentioned. I tell you, it is a treasure.'

'Pa, we saw this picture of you from the early eighties series, and I think I know the people in it.'

'Early eighties!'.

'Yes, Pa, Girish is challenging me. He says. No way I can know them.'

Rahul had some idea of the picture they were referring to. He smiled, the bait has not been wasted.

'Yes, Pa, there is this smart-looking girl with twin plaits standing next to you. Her face is half-turned and in shadows, but I think I know her. I can't place her, but I am definite I know her. Girish and I have a bet going; he says there is no way I can know her; I was not born then.

Shilpa flips through the pages and stops at the large picture dominating the page. It is a picture where Rahul is standing with two girls.

'This is Buajee[22],' Shilpa points out. 'But Pa, who is this girl.'

Rahul looks at the black-and-white picture. He can see the girl's deep blue eyes in the shadows of the black-and-white photo. The half-turned face smiles at him. Rahul knows he can never forget the face, the smile and the eyes.

Sona Na Chandi Na Koi Mahal.

'But Pa, who is this girl? I think I know her. However, I have never seen this picture.'

'Yes, Shilpa, you know her. In fact, I will be surprised in case you don't.'

'See Girish, I win.'

'Okay, you win, but who is she' Girish refuses to give in. 'And how does Shilpa know her? Moreover, how is Dad so confident? Am I missing something?'

'Pa, who is she?'

Rahul is not ready to be questioned. He has been thinking of the answers for too long.

He was happy with the way it was progressing but wanted a wee bit more time to react. However, the

---

[22] Aunt- father's sister.

picture demanded an immediate answer. And Rahul was willing to give one.

'Okay, I will tell you.'

'When Pa?'

'Wait,' Rahul takes his time to light the first and last cigarette of the day.

He is now down to one stick a day after his medicines. A habit he is not willing to give up.

'I will tell you over lunch. Remember to keep some beer in the fridge. Your favourite Sushant *Chachu*[23] will be here, and he may tell the story better. You know the beer he likes.'

'Sure, Dad, done,' Girish smiles. He signals Shilpa to remain quiet. Girish has seen Rahul's fingers slowly caressing the picture. He realises it is more than just a name or a face that Rahul wants to share. And it makes Girish unsure if he has asked the right question. Maybe some questions must not be asked. But the time to think was over. On the other hand, Rahul is happy Girish asked the question; it gives him the opportunity he has been seeking.

The dice has been rolled, and the game is on.

---

[23] Uncle- Father's younger brother.

It is afternoon. Chilled beer is served.
There are four of them. Rahul's dear friend Sushant
and his son Girish
are having Corona with that extra slice of ripe yellow lemon.
Rahul is having his favourite Hayward 5000.
Shilpa is managing the food
and she will take a few sips from Girish's bottle.
Rahul thinks twice and then decides to share the
story of the girl in the picture.
What you read next is the story Rahul and Sushant
shared over a beer that afternoon.

Foundation

People see Rahul as a 'happy-go-lucky' person. Frankly, he refuses to argue with their perceptions because he knows perceptions are always stronger than reality. And if they think so, they must have a reason to do so.

Changing perceptions is really difficult. And Rahul is not bothered by the perception others have of him. Rahul easily adapts to new situations. He believes there are two options in life. You change the other person, or you change yourself. He finds that the latter is more sensible.

Life has been fair to Rahul, yet if he was given a chance to live his life the second time, he would change a few things. You should not be surprised as most of us are never fully satisfied with what life has served us, and given a chance we would want to change a few things.

Rahul has no regrets in the battles called life.

Hayward 5000 is working. Rahul knows he must now pace his beer.

***

Rahul stares at the beer label. He has been silent for a long time, his face flush with the warmness of the chilled Hayward caressing lost memories. The unsaid story tests the audience's patience while Girish, Sushant and Shilpa eagerly wait.

It is important for Rahul to handle the situation well, or there will be chaos, and only he will be responsible for it. If there was anyone who could lose today, it was him.

There were complex unresolved equations and too many variables.

Once the story begins, it will be tough to control the flow of emotions or the narrative. Any damage will be tough to undo. There will be no turning back. Time was running out, and the clock continued its onward journey. No one was willing to stop and give Rahul a few extra moments.

Rahul places the almost empty bottle on the table and gets up. He looks at his closest FFF- Friends for Life – Sushant. Rahul and Sushant have studied together from class 8th. Sushant also knows the girl in that picture and perfectly understands Rahul's situation. Being a part of the family, he has an insider perspective. But today, whatever Sushant says or shares must be timed well. He must wait for his chance.

***

Most Sunday afternoons, Sushant is at Rahul's place. It is a ritual that started after Rahul's marriage and continues till now.

On Sunday afternoons, Sanjana would cook chicken and rice, and Sushant would join them in the afternoon for a few beers. The beer sessions usually finished with lunch. Sushant loved the thick chicken gravy that only Sanjana knew how to cook. Shilpa, Rahul's daughter-in-law, has now mastered the recipe and cooks it equally well.

The beer bottles still get opened most Sunday afternoons. The chicken tastes equally good. And Rahul invariably has to remind himself that Sanjana is no longer with them. Surprisingly, when they remember Sanjana, they all laugh and smile. How quickly have they adapted to the new realities? Sometimes fresh realities need to be invented or crafted. Today, Rahul will need Sushant's help to sort things out. And if everything goes well, Rahul will get what he wants.

The game is on.

***

Shilpa, Sushant and Girish are eyeing Rahul like an accused before the grand jury. Flashback is going to be the chosen platform for conversation.

Today, Rahul is going to talk about the other woman he still craves for.

'Sushant, you tell the kids about her,' Rahul chickens out at the last moment.

'About which one,' Sushant smiles.

Shilpa and Girish look at each other but say nothing.

'About her, about Neeli'.

'Oh Neeli, Rahul, are you sure you want to go down that path? I don't see any logic for you to do so. That is past. A past you never cared for, and I don't see what you will gain'.

'No… Sushant no… there is nothing to hide… and there is nothing to gain. Sanjana was the only one who could be impacted by the story… but then she knew about her… moreover, she is not here… so why not? Maybe it is the right time to tell them about her'.

It seemed Rahul has made up his mind. Truthfully speaking… Rahul felt good about diving deep into their teenage years and remembering her. A different kind of happiness warming him, and it was definitely not beer.

Rahul insists, 'Sushant, I am absolutely sure… you know all about her… and you will see why I am asking you to tell the kids about Neeli.'

Rahul directs Sushant's attention to the album, and Sushant recognises the face in the picture.

Still, Sushant wants Rahul to be sure. 'Ok, don't say I did not warn you'.

There is no reaction from Rahul.

Sushant knows why the album was found today? Why is the picture still there?

Rahul wants him to tell the story.

Sushant tries buying time. 'Before I begin, trust this remains between the four of us.'

'Don't worry… Sushant… you can tell them everything… there is nothing to hide'.

'Damn it, Rahul, it is your story; you should be the one telling it'.

'You start Sushant… I will take over if I feel you are losing the grip… or you are uncomfortable'. Rahul knew Sushant would never say no to a challenge.

'Ok, Rahul, my dear friend, is the hero and the villain of this story. So, here we go'. Sushant looks upwards- as if he was addressing God and telling him - you know I am forced to do this, so take care and help us all.

***

'It is an old story. Some thirty-five or thirty-seven years old. As I tell the story, I know Rahul will relive every moment. I am honoured that Rahul believes I will do justice to the story. He must be right, as I had the best seats in the house most of the time. You know, best friends.'

'Rahul, who you know as a serious type of person, was then a happening dude, an overexcited teenager. Rahul and I shared everything… almost everything.' Sushant paused, smiled and looked at Rahul.

'And for so many years, so many times in the evening, over many drinks, Rahul and I have gone down memory lane multiple times. The story has remained unchanged. I have a request here, please do not ask me questions, or I will lose track, and don't blame me if the story remains incomplete.'

'I am unsure if Rahul realises what he has asked me to do. Past has pregnant pauses, monologues full of unexplored unsaid intentions. Hopefully, I will do justice to the story. Anyway, Rahul, feel free to intervene if I lose track of the timeline or the emotions. It will be of great help.'

'You, Girish and Shilpa are mere props or, shall I say, mute captive audience. But without you, the story may remain incomplete. It is a North Star story; nothing has changed. As a storyteller, my position is tricky. But then Rahul, what are friends for.'

'*Wah Bhai wah*[24], *what say Chachu,* full foundation,' Girish Interrupts.

'Don't listen to him, just continue… I must say, *chachu,* you are a great storyteller.' Shilpa adds.

Sushant ignores the comments and continues.

'Well, there have been evenings when Rahul has sketchily stitched together broken pieces on the canvas of his dream. Every time we find a new emotion or possibility. Don't be surprised if you find traces of yourself in a few episodes of this very natural human story.'

'There is another secret I must share before sharing the story. I have been writing this story with permission

---

[24] Appreciation- a way of saying excellent- you surprise us- was not.

from the main characters, and I know it is a perfect story. Finally, one day, I will be a published author with this one. Maybe some channel could make a series on it. Like every other story, a few names have been changed; they had to be changed. The manuscript is almost ready, and I am only waiting for the final permission from Neeli. The reality is only known to Rahul, Neeli and me. Shilpa and Girish, you don't have to worry about what is true and what is fictional as you get the true version.'

'Wow, Dad, it seems this is a big story... what say, shall we call India TV[25].' Girish jokes, *'Yeh Saksh Joh AAP Dekh Rahey hai Uska Aasli Chera Janiyeh*[26] *,' he delivers the line in typical Saavdhan*[27] India Style.

'Shut up, G,' Shilpa says, 'Or Arnab[28] of Republic TV will join the debate. After all, The nation wants to know- who is Neeli.'

Sushant smiles. 'Rahul is confused and sometimes wonders if Neeli was real and if he ever loved her.'

'Does it matter?' Rahul counters the statement.

'No, it never did' Sushant's voice carried a tone that said it all.

---

[25] One of the leading News channels on TV in India.

[26] Know the real person behind this mask.

[27] Alert- *Saavdhan* India is also a crime-reporting programme on television.

[28] Arnab Goswami is a famous Republic TV journalist known for the 9 PM debate with 'Nation Wants To Know.'

There is a pause. A deliberate pause. The glasses were empty. Sushant pushed his glass to Rahul; the least he could do was fill the glass. A lot of beers will flow today before the story unveils itself.

'WOW, Dad, not bad.'

'No, Girish, it is different. At one time, the only thing young Rahul was sure of was his desire to be with Neeli. But he was unsure if it was love.'

'If that was not love… what love is or… what was that' Rahul was getting high.

'How many,' Shilpa asks and gets no answer.

'So, no, there was more to it… maybe not… to tell you the truth… I am not sure if it was love.' Rahul defends himself and continues. 'It was never a subject of discussion…. It's a fact. I liked Neeli… I dreamt of growing old with her… And I believe the feeling was mutual. But… things happen, or they don't… events need no explanation… life continues... As they say in the Axis Bank commercial… because there is no interval in life.'

'So, Girish, before you ask, let me tell you, it was destined to happen. Losing sometimes can be a great teacher… you have to experience it to believe me.'

Rahul is warming up to the discussion, 'Sushant tells me, you learn a lot when you lose… sometimes, it makes you a better human being. How you react is really your decision… But how do situations react to your decision... you can never be sure. Well, love is known to have an intoxicating effect on people.'

Rahul takes a sip of beer and waits for Sushant to continue.

***

'There is one more aspect of life we must address and lay to rest before I start sharing the real story.' Sushant spoke with some urgency and got everybody's attention. 'Rahul is not the only one who has read the manuscript. When I shared it with some friends, they doubted it was my story. Let me make it clear. I am just the observer. I remember, one day, Rahul asked me if I was in love with Neeli or if I was also interested in her, and I refused to answer. And, if he were to ask that stupid question again, my reaction would be the same. I will refuse to answer.'

'Dad, this is getting interesting.'

'Well, Pa, this is just great,' Shilpa joins Girish.

'As Rahul has asked me to tell the story, I will tell it from his perspective and continue to remain an observer. Treat timelines as props to fix the chronology. If you find it silly, don't laugh. If you find it sad, don't weep. And in no way judge anyone; Rahul or Neeli. Things happen in life. And life is the biggest serial you can binge watch.'

Shilpa and Girish were hooked on the story, and Sushant had their attention.

Sushant adds the final information. 'We, Rahul and I, know where Neeli is. We have met her many times, and Rahul has met her more than I ever did. But, if anyone has met her more than him, it is Shilpa.' Sushant delivers the punch before starting the story.

*Today, I will share the story of Rahul, age 60, a resident of
Defence Colony Delhi. I have no intention of
keeping you waiting....
Here is your turn to flip through the pages of an uncensored
version... as a voyeuristic spectator...
settle down in your ringside chair...
and get ready to travel through my life...no...
Neeli and Rahul's Life....
Unfortunately, you will have to accept
every incident as real...
you have no option...
Only Rahul and Sanjana, or maybe I know the truth ...
and perhaps it no longer matters!
And here is Rahul's story ...*

35 YEARS BACK

PART-II

FLASHBACK

You get to know Rahul's story in detail.

However, Girish, his son and

Shilpa, the daughter-in-law

get to hear only the abridged censored version.

Sometimes. It is nice to be conservative.

Encounter

It is February. Agra has already seen the peak of winter. Slowly one can feel the approaching summer. The weather changes every day. By the time one gets used to getting up late in winter, it changes. The warmness starts increasing. The slow transition of Surya, the Sun-god, starts with Makar Sankranti or Uttarnaryan[29]. However, the impact is felt around Holi[30].

***

Young Rahul was planning to sleep till late, but his mother had other ideas. Netra Sharma never allowed her kids to sleep till late, and that's how it has been in her home. Whereas the new generation Rahul never understood the reason for this hurry. But he had no say in the situation, as Netra Sharma decided how the home would be run, who would do what, and when.

It's 8:30 am, and the Sun is already warming up sleepy lethargic Agra. By the time Rahul finished his morning rituals, the breakfast was ready. A leftover bread from last night rolled

---

[29] Traditionally celebrated when the Sun (Narayana) starts moving towards the northern (Uttar) hemisphere.
[30] Festival of colour celebrated in India sometime in March.

with fresh milk sprinkled with cubes of processed white sugar.

Rahul quickly finishes eating and rushes to the bus stand to catch bus number 131 to Aram Bagh[31]. His college is a few hundred-meters away from the Aaram Bagh bus stand. The college is a welcome escape as the time stretches with his friends like Sushant, and there is no one to tell him what to do.

At college, his favourite game is Time-pass. It has no rules, and no equipment is needed. The game is best played over tea, supplemented with hot Samosa. All one needs is a few friends and some interesting topical, preferably controversial subject to talk about.

Yesterday, the discussion centred around Madam Biswas, their Thermodynamics teacher who is a rumoured lesbian. And the second hot topic was how West Indies bowlers were making life miserable for the Indian team. Sometimes, you don't even need a topic to discuss to kill time.

***

Rahul's father works in a Government department, and the income is limited. As a result, Rahul's pocket money is also limited and insufficient to fund his smoking Wills Navy Cut. Hence, he borrows a few puffs from friends and never smokes an entire stick. Sharing is caring.

---

[31] Bagh= garden Aram = rest-Aram Bagh is a garden- and the name of the locality surrounding it.

Rahul does not carry a tiffin to college. However, the pocket money is enough for him to buy *Bedhmi-Puri*[32], Kachori or Jalebi in the afternoon with a kadak[33] steaming tea at Burman Dada's tea stall. Burman da Tea is excellent and served hot, but you cannot beat what you get in *Kullad*[34] near Sanjay Palace.

Many tea stalls are near the college gate, but the Burman Dada tea stall is the students' lifeline. It is always crowded. The magic is Kishore Burman, the big-bellied Bengali who welcomes everyone with a smile and serves fast and hot. To top it, he allows credit, making him the favourite of hostellers who live from money order[35] to money order. There are legendary *bahikhata*[36] *at Burman da tea stall,* and many accounts are maintained orally. Even the students who have not cleared their past dues are served. On the other side, some students willing to pay in cash are not entertained at the Burman Dada Tea stall. The right to be served is reserved at Burman da Tea Stall.

The tea stall is a basic *Tapri*[37], a small makeshift shed with mud walls further covered with old cloths. Besides being the place where heated debates happen over tea and Samosa, it is a sacred place of learning. A place where you can learn about things in life. Who are

---

[32] Speciality snack of Agra.
[33] Strong- made with more tea leaves and boiling them for a long time to get that dark tea.
[34] Earthen Glass.
[35] A way of receiving money from home through a Post Office delivery.
[36] Indian name for the book of accounts or ledger
[37] Roadside temporary shop.

your friends? What is happening at the university? Who is doing what? Is the new movie worth watching? Is the newcomer committed to a relationship? In fact, during exam season, you can even get coached on subjects and, if you are lucky, get a set of questions that are sure to come in the examination.

Burman Tea Stall silently witnesses all good, bad, ugly, and agitated discussions, deep-rooted confessions, suspected rumours, unnecessary fights, college elections, rowdy non-vegetarian jokes, and the possible exam paper leak. There are many secrets that Burman da would be aware of but does not share. With time, Burman Dada has extended his simple shed, and it now has spacious seating in front and a room at the back where the Burman family lives.

After his last tea of the day, Rahul moves to the bus stop, which is identified by the metal board nailed to the big Mango tree. The bus frequency is unpredictable, but there is no other economical alternative for local transport.

***

Today, the sky is cloudy, and the evening is yet to set in.

Rahul reaches home around 1730 Hours. The moment he opens the creaking metallic gate leading to the stairs of his house, his walk and personality flip. It is true for most teenagers in India, and more so in smaller towns. The gate is the nodal point of transformation as if it is a time vortex.

Rahul's behaviour changes twice a day. He is an extrovert, the centre of attraction at the college, and a disciplined mamma's boy at home.

At home, there is no excitement. There are pre-set unspoken rules and unexplained rituals which he follows without questioning. Time has taught him that there is no point arguing such things. The family is orthodox, and for everything, they

have a somewhat half unproved scientific reason.

The discipline code at home defines what not to do but fails to spell out what should/could/can be done. He knows there are still many years before he can question and stretch these boundaries, and he is willing to wait and have no complaints about these practices.

***

As soon as Rahul enters the home, he heads for the bath. In his family, it is one of those unexplained non-negotiable rituals. You come from outside, and you take a shower. The only exception is if you go to a temple, you don't have to bathe on return. It does not matter how far you went or how long you stayed out. In which situations you are expected to bathe is something you learn with experience and plan your day accordingly. So, if you were to go to the vegetable market in the morning, you would take a bath after returning rather than before going to the market.

The lone tap in the small bathroom is designed for water-saving and can die on you anytime. So, before lathering, Rahul ensures there is a bucket full of water in case the tap runs dry. His hands, with uncanny regularity, glide down to his manhood which involuntarily reacts to the unvoiced, trapped thoughts and images, sending him on a rollercoaster ride.

Post the luxurious bath, Rahul zips to the master bedroom with a towel smugly wrapped around his not-so-athletic belly. He has no problem selecting what to wear next, as there is not much to choose from choices. All this while his ears are tuned to the front door expecting a shout from his friends.

Rahul is on the right side of his twenties. But, as with most in small towns and conservative families, he has never been on a date. Dating is not a concept appreciated or understood in Agra. In fact, he never had what one would call a 'real interaction' with a girl, even after studying in co-education. The only girls he has ever spoken to are family friends or acquaintances of the family or classmates.

The college has been a complete let-down as far as girls are concerned. There are only a few girls in Chaudhary Ram Dayal Engineering College. So, his dream of holding the hand of a beautiful girl and sipping coffee at the Indian Coffee house remains unfulfilled.

In Agra, the girlfriend is not a comfortable concept and subject. They just don't exist.

There is no romance in the city of love. Most girls are passive partners in a one-sided love affair. Such affairs are more of a fantasy of the boy than a reality. Often, the girl is unaware of the boy's interest in her.

If any relationship develops, it is kept under layers of secrecy. Usually, such relationships survive as a surrogate family acquaintance, distant relatives, work colleagues, or sister's best friends or best friend's sister.

Agra is that way, compulsively orthodox. An unsupervised meeting between young adults of the opposite gender is not appreciated and is immediately reported to the parents. The girl character gets scrutinised, and rumours start immediately.

Though there are no restrictions in the Sharma *Khandan*[38], society does not give them the freedom to behave differently. Community, after all, is all about traditions and setting examples.

***

Rahul is now ready. He has managed the impossible task of drying with the worn-out blue Bombay Dyeing towel. It has 2-3 months of life left, after which it will most likely be demoted to one of the many *paucha*[39] for the Kitchen. And it may finally retire when it can no longer be used as Paucha.

The master bedroom is with a low ceiling. The *thekedar*[40] has strategically used two large windows to create an illusion of a larger space. But, the illusions

---

[38] Clan, people of the same lineage.
[39] The cloth used for wiping the floor.
[40] Contractor.

come at the cost of privacy. The windows give a clear view of the neighbour's courtyard. During the daytime, they are usually open to allow the Sun into the rooms and conserve electricity. It also means the neighbours have equal visual access to the Sharma family master bedroom.

The room has a bed and a wooden wardrobe threatening to disintegrate. A study table that doubles as an ironing table and a two-in-one dressing table. And right above it, some books are on the open rack.

Rahul can see the idle hand pump in the neighbours' courtyard from the big window. It requires priming every morning. Hence, there is a strategically placed 1000-litre water drum for an emergency. Next to it is the sagging clothesline along the low boundary wall that is only plastered on the outside. The inside wall is made of naked red bricks that remind him of his middle-income status. A gleaming motorcycle that is rarely taken out is perpetually parked in the narrow alley.

One can see a few buildings under construction at a distance. Flats are selling at much higher rates expecting the new Agra-Delhi express corridor to be announced, adding to the accessibility of the area, and the prices will soar. However, that is the future. Agra has heard of it from the time of Shambhunath Chaturvedi of Bhartiya Lok Dal to now when Nihal Singh of the Indian National Congress represents the area. The only thing that has changed is the political parties now promising a six-lane express corridor.

***

Rahul buttons his shirt and takes a sneak peek at Pandeyjee's home. Nothing is exciting or controversial about Pandeyjee's family. No major fights, at least not the ones that can breach the barrier of the single brick walls. No affairs, no eloping teenagers. It is as if Tulsi Mohalla has decided to be a silent observer of the years passing by.

The last exciting thing that happened in Tulsi Mohalla was the selection of Ratna, the daughter of Mr Mukherjee, in the regional kho-kho[41] team. Mukherjee then went around seeking advice from neighbours. It was their way of letting everyone know of his daughter's achievement before it gets covered in the next day's newspaper. To an outsider, it would look like everyone in Tulsi Mohalla had a say in deciding if Ratna should go to Azamgarh for the district trials. Mr Mukherjee was proud of his daughter's achievement and had nothing against Kho-Kho or the shorts Ratna wore in the matches. It was Azamgarh and the possibilities that worried him. But this story and the incident have nothing to do with Rahul.

The other big window in the room opens towards Pinky Aunty's *Angaan*[42]. Rahul can see her spreading

---

[41] A traditional rural game where one team tries catching other team members in a fixed time. It is a kind of Tag game invented in Maharashtra, India.
[42] The uncovered front part of the house.

clothes to dry. She was one with what would, in Agra, qualify as a progressive modern outlook. She has a well-maintained, toned body. People are surprised to know that she is a mother of two. Rahul shifts his gaze. Suddenly Pinky Aunty turns and looks towards the window as if she has felt eyes boring into her. Sixth sense. She tilts her head and glances toward the window in the signature-style shake of her head. The fingers of her right hand move a few strands of stray hair off her cheeks. Rahul feels awkward. He takes a step back and gets away from the open window. It is an involuntary action. Pinky Aunty wears tight hugging clothes, but they are not cleavage revealing type. Her tits are big, the type males fantasise about. Imagining Pinky Aunty's deep cleavage excites every young man who has seen her, including Rahul.

***

While Rahul is busy imagining Pinky Aunty and her cleavage, his sister walks in.

Sisters have an uncanny ability to break the best of the moments. She whispers, *'Bhai Dekha Bahar Kitni Gori Ladkhi Baithi Hai*[43]*'*

Gori Ladki; two simple, powerful words. Strong enough to short-circuit young Indian males' chain of thoughts. 'Gori,' fair is always higher-up in the hierarchy in the fantasy world of an Indian teenager. Gori = fair = beauty; it is that simple. Being fair is the

---

[43] Brother sees the girl sitting in the front room; she is so fair. (Gori-Fair, Ladki- girl).

most desirable qualification in the marriage market. Fair Girls get fair grooms. Every girl wants to be known as Gori, and cosmetics brands, including 'Fair & Lovely' has exploited it for ages. The creams do nothing other than sell a dream.

But who is this *Gori Ladki*? There is no point asking his sister.

***

This is how Sonia-Rahul's story started.

Rahul's sister was just the messenger, and she could not be faulted for what was to follow.

How could she predict the future?

Rahul's family is a middle-class, middle-income, conservative, traditional family where only arranged marriages happen. Sisters play a crucial role in finding and approving the match. They playfully tease their brothers to gauge potential alliance and interest during family functions. On the other side, the brothers are always trying to impress their sister's friends or the daughter of a known family friend. All in the name of friendship. The sleepy town of Agra was no different.

Even if two youngsters do get introduced, they still have a major problem. Where to meet?

It takes ages for them to be confident enough and take the first step to acknowledge their trapped feelings. Love, real or otherwise, remains a case of a hormonal-induced infatuated chemical reaction. Or plain lust.

Social norms demand that youngsters of the opposite gender maintain a dignified distance. As girls attain puberty and boys' voices start changing, they intuitively understand the socially acceptable distance. In such constrained coordinates, love remains an elusive emotion in Agra. Everything about love is wrapped in secrecy in the city of romance- the city of the Taj Mahal.

For most boys, their first crush is their lady teacher or a friend of their sister. At times, half-baked feelings get fuelled due to misplaced misunderstandings. Things turn stupid and result in bloody family feuds. No one wins, but that is not important. What is important is social status needs to be maintained. No one spares a thought about the young lovers. Everyone is confident that the juvenile love or whatever the couple claims will die its natural death. People typically adapt to the situation and demands of the family.

In Agra, the nuclear family is a new concept that has yet to find social acceptance. Hence, in joint families, brothers, sisters, sister-in-law, parents and senior family members define a complex power structure.

Rahul is far from marriageable age, and his sister is in 6th standard. His sister has never spoken to him like this, and she did say the magic word 'Gori,' which made Rahul curious.

She, the girl in question, is sitting in the living room. A door separates the dining area from the living room. A thick Bombay Dyeing[44] curtain loosely hanging on the rods is the only barrier between Rahul and her. These magic curtains were functional to a large extent. They kept the actual condition of the family protected from the prying eyes of the visitors.

There is a gap between the curtain and the door, just enough for Rahul to peep into the drawing room. What Rahul sees takes his breath away. '*Abey Teri*[45],' he mumbles. It is an involuntary reaction.

The Gori girl is sitting cross-legged on the low sofa with her back resting on the blue cushion that has thinned with years of use. There are six cushions of varying sizes and patterns, each a surviving piece from the earlier retired set.

She is facing the main door. Her side profile is visible to Rahul; however, she is unaware of his presence. She is the fairest of all the girls Rahul has ever seen. 'Gori' is an apt term and most likely an understatement used by his sister for her.

***

Girls with fair skin always fascinate Rahul. Let us give the Gori girl a name; Sonia has sharp features, a high cheekbone and lips that are full. She is wearing a white salwar and red kameez with a white-netted dupatta46.

---

[44] A famous brand of dress material.
[45] An expression of being surprised.
[46] A piece of long rectangular scarf or stole, that Indian women put around their necks- primarily meant to cover cleavage.

Her dress complements her looks; she is graceful and has a magnetic aura around her.

Rahul feels he can keep looking at her for ages but fears she will catch him staring. Rahul does not want it to happen. Suddenly the gentle breeze stops, and so do the curtains. Rahul's strategic window to see her is no longer available. He inches closer to the door and hesitates. He wants to see her, and he knows he is unnecessarily hurrying. She won't just disappear. God Tussi Great Ho[47].

***

Agra is a small town with the mentality of an even smaller town. Every girl, other than your mother, sister or blood relative, is an object of undue attention. The male eye routinely bore through the dress with an apparent on-leash lust. And if the girl happens to be fair, men drool, devouring her with eyes. But that is not the case here. Let me return to reality, the drama slowly unfolding in Rahul's home.

***

Rahul has many unanswered questions.

Who is she?

She is not of his sister's age and is too young to be his mother's friend.

Rahul is in a trance. Pure admiration.

---

[47] God, you are great.

No hint of lust or love. That is not to say there is no lust or love.

Rahul is shy but an open-minded person who grew up reading second-hand novels by Harrold Robins picked from the alley leading to Agra jail. Getting them was easy, but reading them without being caught was a different game.

Rahul's parents would have been scandalised if they had seen him reading Harrold Robbins. The Carpet Baggers, The Adventurers, A Stone for Danny Fisher, The Lonely Lady and Stiletto were Rahul's favourites. And they have helped improve his English and made him a bit freer with words while talking to girls. He takes time to open, but once he does, he is fine.

Most parents are comfortable with the idea of their daughter talking to Rahul. After all, he is a studious, well-mannered mamma boy, and that's how people in his Mohalla saw him.

I tell you, perception is always adulterated with reality.

***

So, who is this new ET48?

Has she recently moved into the locality? Then sooner or later, Rahul will find a way to get introduced. But if she is from another part of the town, then he may never meet her again. Agra, the city, dictates what is acceptable and what is not.

---

[48] Eye Tonic is a term teenage males use for beautiful girls. Item and Totta are other terms meaning the same.

He knew his problem. Too many questions but no answers.

Rahul can't just walk in like the English movie heroes and introduce himself. He has seen many heroes confidently walk to strangers in the English movies screened in Liberty Talkies near Aaram Bagh.

He wants to talk to her. She is cute and pretty. He hesitates; it is natural for him to be nervous. He has no experience of introducing himself to a girl.

Meanwhile, his sister steps out of the house, leaving the 'Gori Ladki' and him alone. Is Gori going to wait for his sister to come back? Or is she waiting for someone else?

Rahul's mind hits the pause button, and his legs feel heavy. He is completely rooted in his position. His mind is busy thinking of the next logical move. He knows he is overthinking; overanalysing is a significant problem for him. But this is not the time to get enlightened. This is a simple, straightforward situation.

Time is of the essence. Sooner or later, Gori will leave.

Rahul had been staring at her for ages. It is his home, and he is peeping between the curtain and the door, watching the Gori girl. The situation brings a smile to his face. It is his home turf, and she is the intruder. Hence, he has the right to question her. A voice inside taunts, 'Great, so why don't you go ahead and do that.'

Air is thick with anticipation. The situation was over-dramatised with only two actors on the stage as if someone had paused the play.

Does she know someone else is at home? Must be.

Does she know who all are at home? Maybe not.

Who is she waiting for? ME!! Is she going to wait for his sister to return?

Rahul is thinking of an icebreaker. Honestly, he does not know a line and lacks the experience to guide him. Moreover, social norms about who should initiate the discussion are confusing. It is a stalemate situation.

***

He is still better than other boys, all thanks to the second-hand English novels he borrows from the A.H Wheeler bookstall in the *'Raja Ki Mandi'* railway station. He has some second-hand inferred knowledge. One can buy books from A.H. Wheeler, read and trade them at half the price. Or pay 20 Rs for every novel irrespective of the number of days it takes to read. This scheme is for fiction novels and Film Magazine but not for Manohar Kahaniya and Debonair, the Indian playboy. In the case of Debonair, even the copies are not displayed. You must ask Gyandeep Bhai Saheb to order for you. Debonair, once sold, never comes back in good condition.

AH, Wheeler introduced Rahul to famous novels like Zaher Ke Ghoot, Andha Hatiyaara, Maut Ke Fande by Colonel Ranjit, Goli, Narmedh, Neelmani and Dharmputa by Acharya Chatursen.

Rahul's understanding is borrowed from English movies like the James Bond series and Texas Detour he watched sitting in the front row and praying no one recognised him. Whatever English he knows is what he painfully learnt from English movies and novels.

Movies, novels and dreams have a strong connection.

In dreams, Rahul, the hero, gets down from the car with a swagger. Girls surround him as if he is James Bond. He promises to realise his dreams when he grows up. But that is about the future. Right now, he has a problem waiting to be solved.

'My Name is Rahul, Rahul Sharma' is not impressive enough and does not have the depth of 'Bond, James Bond.' Hey, have I seen you before? So what. Are you waiting for someone? How original. Do you want water? It is more like Rahul wants water.

Nothing is working out. Rahul is trapped with the Gori predator in the living room. He is tense, evaluative, and indecisive. Rahul needs to take control of his emotions. Worrying never worked. But the situation is completely unscripted for him to be confident.

Rahul is like a character who has been pushed on the stage without rehearsals. He needs to stop peeping and announce his presence to the princess.

Time to act. What if she leaves? What if? Rahul literally forces himself into the living room, into her space! Damn it, it is his house.

To appreciate and visualise everything in slow motion, 18 frames per second.

Rahul enters the 10 feet by 20 feet room, cramped for space. Without being told, She senses his presence and turns. In the same movement, she uncrosses her legs, tugs at the bottom of her kurta and pulls it below her knee. Her smile is inviting. However, Rahul is unsure if the smile is directed at him. But then, no one else is in the room, and the smile makes him feel better.

***

Now, see it from Rahul's point of view. Sonia is gorgeous, and that is an understatement! She is beautiful beyond expectations. Rahul sees her up close, and there is hardly any distance between them, no curtain blocking his view. He is awestruck by her beauty. He greets her and fires the silliest of all 'hello.'

She smiles but says nothing.

Now, Rahul is like *Abhimanyu*[49], who has entered the *Chakravyuha*[50] without knowing how to get out of it. For him, it is not an everyday experience. He does what seems logical to him, and he leaves the room!

Sonia is again alone.

---

[49] Son of Arjun in Mahabharata.

[50] An unusual circular battle formation with a multi-layered labyrinth of defensive walls. It was so tough that it was also called – the maze of death, and few warriors knew how to break it, and fewer knew how to come out of it. On the 13th day of the war, Dronacharya designed this formation.

As Rahul steps out of the door, he turns and takes the narrow steps leading to the terrace. The terrace air feels much better, and at least there is no pressure of expectations from the self.

***

Rahul's house is at the end of the lane, providing an unrestricted view of the narrow road leading to the market. Eighteen narrow, rusted iron steps clinging to the outer wall take you to the terrace. On reaching the terrace, one must turn right towards the front of the house. The terrace is a small, hurriedly cemented surface. An uneven less than 2 feet high single brick wall precariously sits on its perimeter; it looks more dangerous than protective. There is a large Peepal tree with branches covering more than half of the terrace.

***

Rahul knows he goofed big time, and what he did was unpardonable. In anger, his fist finds the wall, and it hurts. He comes back to reality. He wants to see her again; that's all he wants.

He has seen her for a fraction of a second, but the image is imprinted in his mind. In the nanoseconds, his mind registered her deep bluish eyes. In her, he saw a sympathetic, over-eager and out-reaching person. Sure, she deserves another chance.

Rahul's male ego realigns the thoughts to suit his emotions.

After a brief moment of hesitation, Rahul returns and enters the house. Her presence makes a huge difference; the room feels different. The walls are brighter, and the curtains are a lot more vibrant. The air is breathable with a hint of jasmine. That is the impact of Sonia's presence.

Rahul is not sure of anything. And one can't blame him for it.

Rahul would have fainted if the impasse was to last any longer. Perhaps the story would have taken a new turn. Fortunately, nothing like that happened. Rahul asks Gori to shift and gets a puzzled look from her. Rahul now has to justify his action inside his home! 'I have to take some books from the closet behind you. For that, I have to move the Pedestal fan. And for that, naturally, you will have to move.'

She kept sitting.

Was she deaf or simply not paying attention? There were just the two of them in the room. He was embarrassed and refused to wait for her to react. He pulls the table, climbs on it and takes out the books. Before she could respond, he hurriedly left the room.

End of a silent movie part-I.

Rahul is back on the terrace and is unsure why Sonia was smiling when he left the room.

***

The last 45 minutes have been adventurous as the tired Sun takes its own sweet time to set behind the distant plateau. Shadows have started to merge into the surroundings gradually. Shades of grey start replacing the crimson red, and soon it will be dark. Behind the river Yamuna, the majestic silent 'Taj' witnesses the initiation of possibly a new love story.

Rahul watches the Sun go down behind the Taj; he has spent many evenings watching this scene. Even in the rapidly darkening space, he can see the faint outline of the Taj. Soon it will be dark, but the outline of the Taj will always be visible to the people of Agra.

***

Rahul notices a movement at a distance. His sister and Sonia are on the road leading to Soami Bagh temple, which is late by Agra standard.

He curses himself. He remembers his sister asking him to join her for the walk. If only she had told him that Sonia was also going, his reaction might have been different. Now, it was too late, and he had missed the opportunity.

His eyes are focused on the slowly dwarfing figures as they move away from his sight.

He does not know Sonia but wants to be with her for some reason. He has blown his first chance to know her.

***

Rahul is surprised by his muted reactions. As the elder brother, he was expected to ask his sister questions. His sister was going for a walk so late! When? Where? With whom? And when will she be back? He would have been with them if he had done what was expected of him. Rahul reminds himself not to decide without knowing the details.

He will soon forget the promise he made to himself.

Is she from Agra? No, most probably not. Otherwise, Rahul would have known her. A beauty like her can't remain hidden in Agra. Knowing that his chain of thinking is useless, he allows the thought to continue.

Did she recently shift to Agra and his locality?

How does his sister know her?

Will he get another chance to see her?

Rahul knows the answers will reveal themselves in time, and he is not in a hurry. The unanswered questions mock him. Yet, he cannot be chasing the answers. Enough things were seeking his attention.

At around 2100 hours, his mother shares the details on the dining table.

Gori Ladki, Sonia is in town for the whole month of February and is visiting her Mamajee[51] Subhash. To put it differently, she- Sonia will be just hundred-odd meters from his place. The exciting thing is that if one makes an extra effort, one can see Subash's home from Rahul's terrace.

Encouraging facts. *God, Tusi Really Great Ho.*

---

[51] Uncle- maternal side- mother's brother.

Luck, it seems, was finally on Rahul's side. Subhash is a family friend and a few years senior to him. Rahul and Subhash are more buddies than *Mama-Bhanja*[52].

Rahul is sure in the coming week, Subhash will see a lot of him.

[52] Maternal Uncle and nephew.

Are all people in Agra so rude and crude?
I was told that there is a smart guy of my age
and I could meet him in that house.
Is this what Agra would call smart? Tongue-tied.
Silly but maybe cute.
I reserve my comments.
Sonia's initial thoughts on Rahul

Introduction

When in love, one sees the loved one everywhere. Rahul had met Sonia for some four minutes, yet her face kept floating before him. He feels her presence everywhere. Does it mean Rahul is in love? Or it is a case of 'Saavan Ke Andhe Ko Hara Hi Dikhta Hai'[53]. Oh, please don't take it too seriously; Sonia will not pop out of the book on Thermal Conductivity by S. K. Nair or from Differential Dynamics, which anyway Rahul hates to read. But he is finding it tough to concentrate. At college, his mind is only thinking of her. He is not his usual self.

***

Rahul moves like a zombie- totally lifeless and aimless. Today seems to be going slowly. He has been waiting for college to end so that he can meet Sonia. Maybe, after that, he will get peace.

After the last lecture, Rahul would hang around at the Burman tea shop for another 1-2 hours on any other typical day. It was done thing, and the gang met for the last few cups of tea without any agenda. The topic of discussion covered everything possible and exciting, like politics, religion, pure gossip and sex.

---

[53] A jaundiced eye sees only yellow

Everyone was an expert on everything, and no one was willing to accept a divergent point of view. Everyone was free to add their two-penny bit without fearing criticism. And if there was any criticism, it did not matter.

Today, Rahul finds the discussion juvenile. He has grown up overnight! He wants to be back home. Truth, he wants to be with Sonia.

***

It is 3:30 in the afternoon when he reaches home. His mother is sleeping. He throws the bag on the dining table, takes a water bottle from the refrigerator, and thinks of his next move as he sips water.

His mother enquires if he is hungry, and as there is no response from him, she goes back to sleep.

Meanwhile, Rahul is in two minds. He knows it is too early to visit Subhash. It will be odd. Anything unexpected is bound to raise questions he may be uncomfortable answering. Rahul must find some excuse and a story to defend his actions. It is definitely not a good idea to visit her at this hour. Rahul is desperate but not stupid. He doesn't want to advertise his interest in Sonia. He will wait. What they say, *'Sabr Ka Phal Meeta Hota Hai'*[54]. From Rahul's point of view, Sonia will have to wait. Do you notice the change? Sonia will have to wait!

---

[54] The result of patience are always good.

Visiting Subhash's home to meet Sonia is out of the question. It will give away his game. It is, anyway, a new experience and feeling for Rahul. A range of unfamiliar emotions dominates his heart and mind. A tense Rahul is not prepared for it. He is sure he will make mistakes.

***

Rahul knows the first impression counts. Yesterday was not a good start. Today, Rahul will try not to repeat the mistake. In fact, he will do something that will help him recover from yesterday's fiasco. One, he will dress appropriately and be presentable. Two, he will shave in the evening! remove the three-day stubble look of Jhakass[55] Anil Kapoor. He believes girls like clean-shaven guys. To be sure, he shaves twice using the 'Gillette Sensor' which magically slides across his face removing any trace of the faintest of the five-o-clock shadow. He tops it with a healthy dose of 'old spice' aftershave. It is his perfume. His confidence is boosted.

He takes time to select what to wear and favours the currently in-fashion Red-and-black shirt with dark black trousers. He pairs them with the smart-looking brown North-star shoes and ankle-high socks. Finally, he wets his hair for that wet Brylcream[56] look. With the

---

[55] Jhakass is a style of dialogue associated with Anil Kapoor- an Indian actor

[56] A brand of hair cream popular in the early eighties

additional 'one-for-the-road' spray of multi-functional aftershave, he is ready to hit Subhash's home.

There is no point in delaying the inevitable.

He covers the short distance between the two houses in a hurry. When he reaches the gate, the last frontier and the point of no return, new doubt creeps up. He starts losing confidence. Is this really the right thing to do? Is he not forcing the situation? He is visiting Subhash's house uninvited and without any agenda. For what? Just to be introduced to her. Should he not wait for an appropriate moment?

It is February, the shortest month of the year. There is no time to waste, and Rahul must act. Still unsure but somewhat confident, he opens the gate and takes a giant step in his life. It is almost like Neil Armstrong's historic first step on the moon. A Giant Step by Rahul Sharma in a territory he knows nothing about.

***

Subash's home, where Sonia lives, is a two-story building like most other buildings in the area. The landlord stays on the ground floor. The first floor is divided into two parts. The front road-facing portion is vacant, and Subhash occupies the other half. A claustrophobic corridor sandwiched between the boundary wall and the house takes you to the back of the house. Then you take the rickety, poorly ventilated staircase to the first floor and land at the highly unimpressive entrance to the two-room space rented by Subhash. There is a bronze-lettered nameplate on the gate, and it reads Subhash Badola.

Subhash is in his late twenties. He and Rahul are more friends than a Mama -Bhanja. Subhash considers Rahul's mother as Rakhi[57] Sister, so Rahul calls him Mama.

Subhash is single. His flat looks more like a hostel. Rahul has never felt the need to knock or ring the bell. But today is different. Things have changed. It is no longer a bachelor's flat. Subhash's sister and her family are there. However, due to sheer habit, Rahul, on autopilot, pushes the door open and walk-in unannounced. He notices *Gori Ladki* at the study table, busy writing a letter on Inland[58]. His unannounced entry is abrupt; she hurriedly gets up and rushes inside. Rahul is only able to catch a glimpse of her dress. There is no one else in the room. The rest of the family must be in the second room, which doubles as a kitchen, changing room and bedroom, as needed.

Rahul notices the room is a lot cleaner. Things have found their designated space. The newspapers are folded and stacked properly. The pens have found a container; they are all together, the calendar finally shows the correct month and the shoes and slippers are

---

[57] Rakhi is a symbolic thread that a Hindu sister ties on her brother's wrist and takes his commitment always to protect her and her honour. So Rakhi sisters are not in blood relation.
[58] These were pre-formatted papers sold by the post office. Once folded along the marked creases and stamped – they could be sent through the post.

neatly placed on a bamboo shelf. The place even smells fresh. Aha, a woman's touch. The gender-racist thought brings half a smile to his face.

***

His guess is right. Subhash is the first to come out with questions in his eyes. What brings you here at this hour? How come? Anything you want? Everything all right? Something special? Rahul is still standing at the door.

Honestly, none of the questions is voiced. So, Rahul is not obliged to answer. He wishes Subhash and sits on the *Diwan*[59]. Like most of the things in the house, Diwan is also multipurpose. It is used for sitting during the day, and if the need arises, it converts into a bed at night. Some storage space is under it, where all the drinks are stacked.

Silence. There is nothing to talk.

Rahul's mind is racing, trying to think of possibilities. He has time on hand.

There is nothing unnatural in the way she left the room. Any girl will do the same. Still, to him, her exit looked odd. It makes him feel like an intruder. Did she see him as some threat?

Life has no rewind button; what is past is gone, and he can do nothing about it. He did walk in unannounced,

---

[59] A multipurpose rectangular long box-type furniture piece used for storing things as well as seating.

catching the young lady by surprise. It was plain stupid of him to do so.

Now, as a damage control, he must engage with Subhash. He likes Subhash, but today his mind is somewhere else; it is as simple as that. In his scheme of things, Subhash is a mere pawn. The conversation is going nowhere. Rahul is not even hearing what Subhash is saying. Subhash's new identity as Sonia's uncle gives Subhash complete freedom to speak uninterrupted, and he enjoys it. Today Rahul is not countering him with his smart ones.

If things move the way he wants, having Subhash on his side will be an advantage. Getting tortured by an irrelevant stupid uninterrupted monologue is a small price to pay.

However, everything has a limit. Rahul gets restless. His eyes keep darting toward the door leading to the second room. To him, it is a barrier, not a gateway. Rahul is here to see Sonia and, if possible, talk to her. It is the area of uncertainty. He is unsure if Sonia would like to meet him, and he can't think of a reason why she should be interested.

Let me simplify the situation by over analysing it.

Rahul wants Sonia to acknowledge his presence and her interest. He is waiting for a signal from her. At least she should say that nothing is wrong. It is absolutely natural for him to expect that.

So, Rahul does what comes naturally to him. He keeps nodding to whatever Subhash says. His ears are pinned to the next room, and he can hear voices he fails to recognise. What he hears is his inner voice shouting, 'Just one glimpse, some sign of interest, And I promise I will leave.' Naturally, there is no response.

***

Subhash works in a Cargo company. He leaves for the night shift at 7 P.M. Soon. It will be time for him to go. Rahul's mission is doomed. If Sonia does not come out by then, Rahul will have to leave with Subhash. Rahul can see the minute hand of the wall clock threateningly moving towards 6:30. Soon, it will be 7 P.M. Then what?

***

Subhash excuses himself and apologetically tells Rahul he has to rush; he is getting late. As an afterthought, he suggests *'Chai Pee Kar Jana'*[60]. Rahul is happy. He has hit the jackpot, opening new possibilities and a chance to meet her.

Subhash leaves.

Now the situation is different.

If Rahul stays and the promised tea is served, Sonia will serve it. He smiles; the wheel of luck is finally favouring him. However, there is a small problem. He still has to choose between waiting or leaving. What if no one heard Subhash suggesting tea for Rahul?

---

[60] Go after having tea

He could hear the second hand of the wall clock announcing the death of every second. He knows he is losing time. Maybe, no one in the other room heard Subhash. *Chutiya*[61]*, saala*[62] *Ladki Patayega, Ishk Fharmayega*[63] Rahul speaks to himself. But he decides to wait.

*****

On the table is a small penholder with colour pens and a writing pad. Rahul has an idea. He pulls the chair and starts drawing faces. The pens are not in the best of condition. However, Rahul manages to find two decent ones. He starts setting up the trap.

When Rahul sketches, he gets in a zone. Smooth, confident, effortless lines start flooding the space. Soon recognisable shapes start emerging. He is good with colours and can draw reasonably well. He enjoys sketching. And it is a trick that has never failed him.

Whenever Rahul wants attention or to impress anyone, he draws. Sooner or later, the person checks what he is doing and is superbly impressed with an expression of disbelief. After some small irrelevant banter, Rahul finds ways to move to a more exciting conversation. It is a trick he has used often.

Rahul concentrates, knowing that the end product must impress her. He does not notice Sonia walking into the room. She pulls a chair and sits close to him.

---

[61] Useless person
[62] A slang- that translates to Wife's brother
[63] You will woo the girl, be romance!

What's on paper is impressive. Rahul continues sketching without acknowledging her presence. His master Sunjit has taught him one guru mantra. *Opportunity create Karo, Bhav mat do- kudh aayegi*[64]. It is counterintuitive, but it works.

'You are Sheela's brother?' she takes the initiative.

It is more of a statement than a question.

'Haa.'

'You are Rahul, Right.'

'Haa,' another monosyllable reply.

Rahul is not a good conversationalist—and terrible when it involves beautiful girls his age. The spontaneity dies. He starts thinking ahead, dreaming of new ways to impress, and in the process, everything is lost.

There is a pregnant pause, a pause, not a complete full stop.

Rahul is nervous and uncomfortable. Unable to do anything else, he gets up, pushes the chair, sidesteps Sonia and leaves the room. He knows it is not the right thing to do. But he is unable to think of anything else.

Rahul does not remember coming down the stairs, walking through the corridor and reaching the rickety wrought iron gate. He should have thanked her for the tea he never tasted.

---

[64] Create opportunities; don't give her more importance, she will come automatically

Rahul turns to close the gate and catches her staring at him. It is spooky; he is not prepared for it. His eyes riveted on her face, a searing pain rips through his fingers, and he returns to reality. He has managed to close the heavy latch on his finger.

Let me freeze-frame the situation.

If this was a scene from Indian Movies, Sonia would have rushed to Rahul's side, fussing over the injured finger. She would look up with pleading eyes blaming herself for the accident. But she just kept looking at Rahul.

Rahul's male ego refuses to acknowledge the lack of sympathy or pain; with *'Mard ko Dard Nahi Hota'*[65] attitude, he leaves. This time, he carefully closes the gate and starts the lonely walk home.

'What the hell.' His fingers were trapped. She saw how painful it was. What kind of girl is she, so cold, no question, no care? What does she think of herself?

***

More unanswered questions than answers.

Why is she in Agra? How will she react to his abrupt exit? Was she at the gate to ensure he left? Did she expect him to go back? Did she want to say something? What if he had continued sketching? The last was an open-ended question, full of possibilities - each scarier than the other.

---

[65] A Man does not feel the pain

Rahul's male ego assures him, that she must be thinking of him. Most likely, she is confused and trying to make sense of things. She may be asking herself, Why did Rahul come? Why did he stay for only a short time? Why did he leave abruptly? She must be trying to guess, just the way he is.

Rahul starts thinking of ways to damage control. He replays the episode frame by frame. But, he is unsure of her interest.

The inflated male ego starts post-rationalising. If Sonia is not interested, why did she come out when he left? Look at it this way. When he was at the gate, she was at the door. Once he left, she came to the gate. Was she checking how stupid he was? Was she blaming herself for the injury?

Rahul's super creative mind was on overdrive.

What should he do next? What will be an inescapable trap? Something that has no chance of failure. What must he do to catch her attention? What will interest her?

One thing Rahul was sure, Sonia was a confident extrovert young beautiful girl. How she pulled her chair, sat next to him and initiated conversation! Initiated conversation!! Almost whispering in his ears. No girl in Agra will ever pull a chair and sit next to a stranger. At least no girl that Rahul knew, and he hardly knew many.

***

Not sure where this whispering in the ear came from. Maybe it was Rahul's imagination. Or was he reading too much in every small gesture? No amount of concentrating and visualising it in slow motion was helping the situation. It is going to be a good game.

Time-pass! Rahul is not looking at her as time pass. But then, how can he be serious about her when he knows nothing? It was indeed Rahul's problem, and only time has the answers.

What was that?
I am intrigued by what happened.
Silly, introvert guy. I know, he will come around.
I know he came to meet me; otherwise,
why would he stick around after Mamajee left.
For tea!
Give me a break.

- Sonia

Another Day

Nothing has changed. The world is still the same. Yesterday Rahul was this close to Sonia before he left abruptly. Something he knows he should not have done.

Every day brings with it a new set of challenges.

Today, Rahul is unable to focus on anything. His mind is busy conjuring future possibilities banking on the optimism that always worked for him.

She pulled her chair and sat next to him. That was cosmic bliss till he blew it.

She was close enough for him to see the tiny mole under her chin. The uncalled-for closeness unsettled him. He likes to be in control.

In his dreams, Rahul's virgin arms hug her.

You understand what it means. Yesterday, his walking out was an act of cowardice.

He consoles himself; Things will get better. They always do.

***

Rahul has no idea what could have happened if he had stayed back. He is an optimist and only sees positive possibilities. In Agra, the dreams of teenagers are constrained by societal norms, although no one monitors them. But, people dream within their *Aukat*[66], and *sometimes they forget it.*

Rahul wished the social norms were more relaxed. Wishing was all he could do.

He considers the unlimited possibilities. In case of an adverse reaction, he must consider all the options, including honourable escape. He must ensure there is no mistake and no failure. If it sounds like a complicated thing to do, it is complicated, at least for him.

Rahul is into uncharted territory with possible negative backlash. A wrong step can damage the family image. Sonia is an unknown element, and he knows nothing about her. The only thing that matters is that he wants to meet her.

Rahul's short-term goals are simple. He must get properly introduced and get familiar with her. Maybe be friends. Maybe go for an evening walk and have *GolGappa*[67] at the *Kallu Pani Puri* near *Barhan Tiraha,* just to make his friends jealous.

*****

It is already 11 A.M. Rahul has no clue how the day will progress. Time seems to be flying. Rahul gets up

---

[66] Capability, but mainly used as status in society. A complex of capability, capacity and social standing.

[67] Also called Paani Puri. It is a famous Indian snack. It consists of a round, hollow puri, fried crisp filled with flavoured water, tamarind chutney, chilli, chat masala, potato, onion or chickpeas.

and glances through the headlines in the newspaper. Nothing new. Amar Ujjala, Agra edition is filled with political news and some jokers making promises he never intends to fulfil. Sports pages are covered with the upcoming West Indies cricket series. Local pages devoting extra space to hyperlocal events, a few protests, a case of eve-teasing near SRK Girls Inter College at Khandari and a fire near *Raja Ki mandi*[68.]

Picking his notebooks, he rushes to catch the city bus. As usual, the bus is crowded. He smiles at the twin Tiwari sisters. It is tough to tell them apart. He wonders what will happen if they get married in the same house. Only they would know who they were sleeping with. Maybe the husbands won't even mind. But what if the husbands are also twins? Damn, Tiwari Twins are beautiful. But Sonia is leagues ahead.

He gets down at the college and is in no mood to attend classes. For him, the rest of the world does not exist. His mind is preoccupied with his problem. What should he do? Maybe there is a way out. Perhaps he should just go with the flow.

***

Sometime during the day, he decided to bunk the rest of the classes and go home. Sonia is on top of his mind, and he has been thinking about her. He is yet to find a way out. He walks on autopilot and knocks at the door, only to realise too late that he is knocking at the wrong door. It is He is Subhash's home. He was not supposed

---

[68] Suburban/extension railway station of Agra

to be here. He should have been at his home. It was too late to back out. Now, he needs to play this one by ear. He sure will find a way out. He has been in more hopeless situations than this. He will manage, and he knocks again.

*****

In 8th standard, pushed by friends, Rahul wrote his first love letter. It is addressed to Anita, a girl in his class. Was that her name? The name is not important. If you ask Rahul, he will tell you Anita's smile fooled him, and he misunderstood her genuine frankness as an interest in him.

Give Rahul the benefit of the doubt. He was a curious kid in 8th standard and just thirteen. It is when the kids start learning how the babies are made and get exposed to lovemaking and sex. And anyway, while growing up in Agra, the concept of genuine frankness and an innocent smile did not exist. Only when he started working did he realise things were not always how they looked.

It all started with a simple incident.

One rainy morning, Anita and Rahul, who lived on different sides of the town, were coincidentally late reaching school. They were thoroughly drenched. The class teacher Madam Tandon excused them from the assembly and told them to go to the classroom and try drying their uniform.

The glass-doored almirah was full of books and divided the classroom into two sections. In one section, the students attended classes, and the other was an unused annexe. The classroom was earlier a library, and while the library shifted to the new building, a few old almirahs cramped with books were left behind. Rahul was sure these were the old books no one wanted to read, and maybe they were no longer in the library records.

He sat in the classroom, wondering what to do when he accidentally saw Anita through the gaps between the almirahs. She had removed her white top and was trying to dry it in the annexe. His back was towards the almirah. To get it right, think of Rishi Kapoor watching Simi Grewal in Bobby. It was the first and the last time Rahul had seen a female classmate changing uniform. He stood rooted to his place. Her Tunic covered part of the back, yet his young mind could not help imagining. After putting on her half-dry top, she returned to the classroom side, where she saw young Rahul still in his wet shirt. She volunteered to help dry it.

Later during the lunch break, Rahul shared the incident with his friends. He added *mirch masala*[69] to make it spicy. His friends read too much into the incident. Their unanimous verdict was simple and innocent. Anita is interested in him, and she is giving all the signals, and only Rahul cannot decode them.

---

[69] Adding spice to the story.

Otherwise, what was the need to volunteer to help to dry his shirt?

Rahul Phass Gaya Yaar[70]. It was not an isolated incident. A lot many innocent acts were remembered and re-interpreted by his friends. Some said she is from an army background, and don't we all know how open they are? Every girl has boyfriends. And there was that extra weight to the 's' at the end of the boyfriend. And we all know what boyfriends do or want. Soon Anita became Paro and Rahul Devdas. How was poor Rahul at that stage to know it was just a one-sided affair and that there was no Paro?

Rahul's impressionable mind and infatuated heart got confused.

It was clear. He was the boy, and it was for him to act.

It is what led to Rahul writing his first love letter. Then he waited for the right moment. In between the classes, when teachers were moving from one class to another when the students and the classrooms were totally unsupervised, Rahul tossed the neatly folded love letter to Anita.

Sometimes timing is all you need. His timing was terrible.

The letter was arrested mid-air by the PTI (Physical Training Instructor), who was on his post-lunch rounds. It created a huge ruckus. It was the first love letter in the history of the school. No, there is no honour roll for

---

[70] Rahul, you are trapped.

such courageous deeds; otherwise, Rahul would have made it to the esteemed list.

The PTI beat the hell out of Rahul. He used his hands and then the sleek cane that hurt a lot.

In those days, capital punishment in school was an acceptable and often encouraged way to enforce discipline. The PTIs were de facto the head of the discipline squads. Rahul convinced the PTI that it was a juvenile mistake and never happen again. For no known reason, PTI dropped his demand to call the parents for a meeting. And as luck would have it, most in the school heard of the case as a rumour but never knew who wrote the letter.

That is some glorious past to benchmark with.

***

Sonia opens the door.

'Hello,' Rahul is tentative.

'Hi,' she answers in a flat tone. There is no emotion, threat, question, invite or complaint.

'Is Subhash in?'

'NO!!'

Was there a tinge of surprise in her voice? Or was she irritated? Maybe she had been sleeping, and Rahul disturbed her. Or perhaps she was expecting Rahul, and his asking for Subhash was the irritant. Was Sonia expecting Rahul to explain his behaviour? Maybe. Should Rahul say sorry? Maybe.

One will never know, but Rahul had a feeling that Sonia knew he was at the door before opening it. Rahul had not learnt his lessons, and he was again reading too much in an innocuous situation. He should avoid equating politeness to interest.

'Just tell Subhash,' Rahul turns, even before completing the sentence. The message was meaningless. It was not Subhash he had come to meet.

'Won't you come in?' Rahul is surprised and not sure If he heard her right.

Rahul takes two-and-a-half steps to change his status from unsure-uninvited to an arrived guest. His mind is racing through the spectrum of possibilities. It always does. Last evening, she was so close to him in this very room, and he had left.

There is a surprise waiting for him. The whole family, i.e., Sonia's younger brother Ajay and her mother, are dressed up. It is clear they are going out, and Rahul feels unwanted. It is not the time to test the Indian ethos of 'Atithi Devo Bhava'[71].

'Oh, I will leave; it seems you all are ready to go somewhere.'

Sonia smiles. He is ready to be the clown if she continues smiling like that. Her eyes twinkling with expectation. He is trapped. No way he can walk away two days in a row. She then tells him that the family was anyway on the way to his house. Rahul looks at

---

[71] A philosophy that means the guest is like God.

the *Saraswati Mata*[72] picture on the wall calendar and raises his eyebrow to say, *'God Tussi Great Ho.'*

This was double luck. His house! They are coming to his house. He has no interest in Ajay and his mother. For him, they were unnecessary baggage. Now he will have the home advantage. For a change, he smiles as he leapfrogs into his imaginary world of probabilities and possibilities. Logical, rational thoughts laced with emotional earthquakes thunder through his mind. It is an opportunity he cannot afford to lose.

***

It is Rahul's house where the first episode of this crazy story was enacted. The house at the intersection of *'Strand Road'* and *'Pandit Kali Charan Tiwari Road'* is easy enough to find. His home follows the template of most of the houses on the east side of Soami Bagh temple.

A two-story building. The landlord stays on the ground floor. The first floor is accessed by climbing short compact 23 steps. As you reach the small platform - 5 feet by 6 feet- two doors lead to two portions. The door on the right leads to Rahul's house, and if you continue on the steps, you will hit the terrace.

***

Rahul starts walking with the family. Sonia, however, slows down, allowing others to lead. Rahul follows her

---

[72] Hindu Goddess of knowledge.

like a puppy. He sees her free-flowing blue *dupatta* fluttering in the windy evening. It brushes his face – and that is the filmy moment of the day, almost like Sridevi's extraordinarily long *pallu*[73] brushing against Anil Kapoor's face in *Lamhe* or Sushmita Sen's *pallu* wrapping Shahrukh Khan's face in *Mai Hoon Na*. So romantic.

Sonia pulls her dupatta and wraps it around her face. Game over.

Even though Rahul and Sonia were walking behind, they didn't walk close to each other.

There is no traffic. Some kids from the neighbourhood are busy playing cricket. The batsman strikes the ball, and it comes in their direction; Rahul catches it without breaking his stride and throws it back in one smooth action, which lands into the wicketkeeper's hands. Natural reflex, and Rahul, at least today, does not mind showing off.

They reach their destination. Rahul rings the bell and then realises it is his house. Sheepishly he pushes the door. He makes the family comfortable in the small living room with more props than sitting space. The old sofa can seat three uncomfortably, a glass coffee table that is too big for the room, an almirah with transparent doors that is full of books, a few chairs and a diwan. No one is sure where to sit. Finally, Sonia and her mom take the sofa, and her brother takes one of the

---

[73] The end part of a saree is thrown over the shoulder.

chairs. Rahul and his mother end up sitting on the diwan.

Rahul is surprised at how easily the two ladies hit off. They dig out new subjects for conversation and smoothly move from one topic to another. They have common friends and relatives, making the conversation that much easier. Both try demonstrating the width of their network by sharing updated information. Nothing in their conversation interests Rahul, but as he is part of the host family, he can't leave.

What about Sonia? Is she enjoying it?

Rahul looks at her and finds her looking at him. He turns the other way. After a few moments, he looks at her again. Sonia is busy playing with her hair. She is bored and is trying hard to fake interest in the conversation. She shows her indifference with a tweak of her eyebrows and slowly gets up, giving the two ladies enough time to react. As if daring them to question her. Nothing happens, and Sonia steps out of the room onto the platform on the first floor.

***

A 25-watt bulb barely lights the area. Like a lamb, Rahul follows Sonia.

Her *dupatta* is strategically placed to cover her cleavage. She is sensuous, exciting, to be honest, *sex-citing*. He stands there admiring her, not knowing what to do. For the first time, Rahul understands the phrase 'Time stood by.' Seconds seem like hours.

Sonia walked out because she was bored, and now, she was also at a loss, not knowing what to do. Sometime in the future, Sonia will tell Rahul; she was sure he would follow her. The spark in Rahul's eyes when she opened the door at her home had given away his interest. She smiles and looks at Rahul. The silent question 'Now, what ?' hangs between them.

Rahul knows he is expected to lead.

It was not going as per the script.

'Terrace chale'[74], Sonia says. It is neither a request nor a question. It seems like an order. Rahul follows.

The street light partially lights the terrace, and the part away from the main road is somewhat dark. A prolonged silence punctuated with the soft rustle of peepul leaves in the background.

It is for Rahul to break the silence.

Rahul wants to know about her, so he must first start the conversation. Maybe ask some open-ended questions without sounding suggestive.

So, Rahul asks Sonia, Where do you stay? He realises it was a stupid question. But it was a start.

'Nanital'[75].

A Monosyllable response is like a checkmate in conversations. It is again Rahul's turn in the game of 'come, let's know each other.'

---

[74] Let us go to the terrace.
[75] A famous hill station in Uttarakhand.

'You are Subhash's cousin,' Rahul ventures into unknown territory. He knew it was not true, but then it was good to check, or soon he may be calling her Mausi[76.]

'*Dhut*[77], he is my Mamajee.' That *dhut* was so passionate, so romantic. It was delivered with a high level of comfort and openness. Rahul smiles, but frankly, he is still not comfortable with the situation, and one of the reasons for his discomfort is his being alone with a Gori Ladki or any girl.

Rahul curses himself; what an idiot he is. Why can't he think of something pleasant, positive and comforting? He is wasting the opportunity when he has her undivided attention.

Rahul senses that Sonia is evaluating while he is busy thinking of something interesting that could qualify as a decent conversation starter. Exciting and engrossing, lively enough for the lady to be interested in.

The pause is stretched longer than expected. Rahul considers asking her, 'What's your name?' He realises that will be blunt. One does not ask a girl her name just like that. 'May I know your name?' sounds prude as if he was a kindergarten kid seeking the teacher's permission to go to the washroom. Finally, he decides to ask her simply, 'So, what's your name?' It sounds informal, and he can always add, 'My name you already know.'

---

[76] Mother's sister.
[77] Affectionate way to tell someone don't be silly.

'Sonia, Sonia Jhakmola, well you could call me Neeli, that's what all my close friends call me, it's a lot more informal.'

Sonia did not ask Rahul anything, and it hurt.

Did they come to the terrace to have a unidirectional interrogation?

'You know my name, but you can call me Sippy' It took Rahul all the courage to share his nickname. It is so feminine sounding that Rahul hates anyone calling him by his nickname. But he makes a special concession for Neeli.

'Only two of my friends, Sadhana and Madhulika, call me Neeli, and now you too can,' she stops.

Rahul feels honoured to be included in the list of close friends. He is cautious; there is no need to be super excited. Sonia fails to notice the wave of happiness on Rahul's face.

And silence prevails on the dim-lit terrace.

Sonia stands facing Rahul, but he cannot see her face clearly as she has her back to the streetlight, the only light source. However, Rahul is facing the streetlight, and Sonia can see every expression playing on his face.

It is not a position of advantage. But Rahul knows how to manoeuvre it with some deft movements. He moves toward the staircase and then, as an afterthought, turns back. Sonia has meanwhile turned to follow him, and then she too stops. Rahul manages to change positions and is more at ease.

'Do they call you 'Neeli[78]' because of your beautiful eyes?' Rahul completes the rest of the thoughts in his mind. Your eyes are so deep… what they say royal blue… no Persian blue.

'You will have to ask my mom about it.' She continues, 'But I am told during birth, for some complication, my body had a blue tint … lack of oxygen or something… and my grandfather is rumoured to have said… Neeli… now with this colour of eyes (she fluttered her eyelashes), the name stuck.'

Simple explanation.

'I don't think names have any mystery around them… they just stick… tell me why people call you Sippy… so cute a name.'

Rahul was not surprised; his nickname never failed to raise curiosity. There has to be a story for a handsome dude like him to get a name like Sippy! 1 Sharing nicknames worked for Rahul.

'It's a long story… I am not sure you want to know.'

Sonia did not react. So, he went ahead with the story that has been traded many times.

---

[78] Neela in Hindi means blue coloured, and Neeli would suggest one who is blue.

'I was born and brought up at *Kanpur*[79]... and when I was 3-4 years old, there used to be this girl living next door... we were great friends, always playing together, or so I have been told... Her name was 'Simple Kaur,' and she was called 'Sippy.' It started as a tease; senior members of the family joked about our pairing and that we should be married when we grow up. Always commenting on our hunger for each other's company. In the process, somehow, the name got pasted on me too... and that's what it is.'

'Do you know where that girl is now' she countered.

'No.'

It was the first time someone had asked him this question... it made him think. Was Sonia so interested in him... there cannot be any other explanation for her asking such a personal question... well, good luck ... thank you, Sippy Kaur.

Rahul faintly remembers the pony-tailed face of a chubby girl from some photographs. Frankly, he was clueless about where Sippy was. Most likely, if they would cross each other on the street, he will fail to recognise her.

The good thing is that Sonia and Rahul were finally having a decent conversation. The next few minutes were lost in sharing more details. Sonia was doing 'Political Science,' 1st year of the 10+2 system from 'St.

---

[79] Big town in Uttar Pradesh. Famous for leather goods and fabric. It was also called Manchester of East.

Mary & Joseph College' at Nainital and was waiting for the first-year results. Rahul, as we all know, is a first-year Engineering student.

However, everything was not fine.

Rahul and Sonia were poles apart. She is religious… he is a rationalist… she likes and respects Indira Gandhi as a leader… he is in awe of Margaret Thatcher… She believes in Palmistry, and for him, that is one way to hold the hands of beautiful girls. She likes what he hates, and so on. Hold on, don't opposites attract! How does it matter? It is not that they are getting married.

The stage is set. The character and cast assembled. It now depends upon Rahul's actions in the next 25-26 days. It is definitely getting interesting.

Sonia is looking at him and is lapping every word. When they are warming up to each other's company, his sister comes and breaks the magic spell. Sonia and Rahul were wanted downstairs.

The tea is served.

They have no option but to join the rest of the crowd. The elders are enjoying the relative comfort of having common friends. Young Ajay is the odd person out. There is no one of his age group, so he is busy reading a *Chacha Choudhary*[80] comic. Sonia and Rahul have to sit through the pointless conversation, but at least they acknowledge each other presence with knowing smiles.

---

[80] A famous comic book character known for his wisdom.

As if on cue, everyone thinks it is getting late. Sonia and Rahul are surprised. Sonia's home is hardly 60 meters, and it is not too late. Rahul and his mother stand at the door, and their eyes follow the guest for different reasons. They watch until the guests take a turn and are out of sight.

***

Show over. Rahul goes to sleep thinking of Sonia.

Not bad. Rahul is a sweet cute guy.
Not very talkative and hell he takes a long time to warm up.
The rest of the month could be fun here at Agra.

- Sonia

So Far

Rahul feels fresh and charged up. Nowadays, he thinks of Bina a lot less. Bina has been Rahul's centre of attraction for the last three years... till Sonia made her entry. ... Rahul in some way thinks he belongs to Bina, and she has many times given hints of her interest. There are unsaid promises but no commitment.

Nothing wrong.

Rahul tries rationalising his behaviour. He questions himself. Is this right- what he is doing? How can he be so indifferent to what Bina thinks? Since Sonia has walked in his life (wow, walked in his life!). She is the face he wants to look and talk to.

What if Bina meets another guy... and behaves the way he is behaving ... will Rahul accept it? The answer is NO. The terrace of her house is much larger than Rahul's. What if right now there is someone with her on the terrace, just the way he was with Sonia.

Rahul hates such thoughts.... but the possibility exists and he can't deny it. Why can't he be carefree like his friends? Say like Sunjeet or Vikas. Why does he have to over analyses everything? Rahul knows that has been his problem. And anyway, there are no promises and commitment in one-sided infatuation.

***

This is not the right time for analysing feelings. He will cross the bridge when the time comes. The mind is a restless organ; it vacillates till it is forced to take a decision. The mind does not differentiate between reality and fantasy. It is trained to evaluate possibilities and options. Unfortunately, when faced with the Good, Bad and Ugly, it picks the worst possibility. The brain is wired that way. It follows the first principle of survival. In the process, it gives birth to new problems.

Bina will have to wait. And how is she going to know what is going in Rahul's life and mind? And even if she knows, what is the problem. They are only comfortable with each other- just friends.

***

Today is Sunday and Rahul is home alone. There is no cricket practice, no match, no friends to visit and nothing to study. He is waiting for a signal from Sonia. His male ego reassures him, Sonia craves his company and then there is no one else in the town she knows. She studies in a convent school, maybe she would be looking at some spicy stories of her vacation to share with friends when she goes back to Nainital. *Woh Jawani bhi kya jiski kahani na ho*[81].

---

[81] What is the youth, which does not have a story to tell?

104

Throughout the day, Rahul makes umpteen visits to his terrace. Every time hoping that he could spot Sonia. There is no signal. It irritates him, but he can do nothing. He decides that he cannot visit her unannounced or uninvited. Otherwise, she will know he is chasing her and the effect she has on him. Visiting unannounced is ruled out.

***

What if Sonia is waiting for a signal from him? The possibility cannot be ruled out. She is a young, innocent girl in a new town. Does Rahul really expect her to signal? A girl to take the initiative! The wait is going to be really long. However, this time Rahul is willing to play the patience game.

***

By 2 P.M., the situation becomes unbearable and it makes Rahul restless. By 3 P.M. he is a nut case. Unchartered irrational thoughts flood his mind. He knows Sonia is in town till the end of February, the shortest month. It is possible, that Sonia and her family may have other plans, after all, it is their first trip to Agra, the city of love- the city of the Taj Mahal.

There is another possibilities that trouble him more. What if Sonia is unwell? Has the family gone somewhere? A lot of maybe's clutter his head while he seeks certainties and solutions. He continues making frequent trips to the terrace, just in case. Even though he knows that it will have to be a brilliant coincidence of her and him being on the terrace of their houses simultaneously. The probability is more of them missing each other. But then *Dil toh bacha hai, dil toh saccha hai*[82].

Surprisingly, no one is talking about Sonia and the family. Usually, his mother would do the post-mortem of anyone visiting them. Tell the family, what she found good or bad with the visitors, but today she is silent. Rahul is not sure, if he should read more in this behaviour of his mother.

He waits. Finally, the police-line clock strikes eleven in the night. Rahul is a destroyed man. His confidence is at rock bottom. Physically tired, mentally fatigued with conflicting emotions, he sleeps the moment his head hits the pillow.

In the dreamland, the wait is over. Sonia comes to meet him. Silently she sneaks next to him. They are alone, and she looks more beautiful than ever. Rahul looks deep into her intoxicating eyes. He wants to complain about the day, about the wait, but Sonia places a finger on his lips and Rahul forgets all his problems.

---

[82] The heart is innocent like a kid and honest.

Today been a longest and boring day.
What could have kept him busy?
Is there something wrong? Is everything fine?
I will only know tomorrow.
I have been at home all the time.
The family had no plan but to rest at home.
And the silly boy never came.

- Sonia.

Eventful Day

A night of good sleep is the best cure for emotional tension. A 6-8-hour rest can relax and maybe help attack the problem afresh. And even the dreams may give you a clue – the key to the problem. Dreams can be a problem or even a solution.

***

Rahul is annoyed. Come to think of it, he wasted an entire Sunday for her.

So, if Sonia wants to play the game, she will get what she deserves. She will have to wait. She is not the only skirt in town for him to chase. If she wants his company… it will be on his terms… she will have to come and beg… she will have to seek him out and plead for forgiveness.

Rahul smiles at the most positive thoughts of the day. It makes him feel better. Rahul enters the shower and is ready for the battle.

***

Rahul has to walk to *Chhaala Road* to catch the Rickshaw. And on the way he must cross Sonia's house. He decided not to look in that direction. There was nothing to interest him. However, since Sonia is on his mind, things are a wee bit different. A few more steps and then he will take the turn, her house will get out of sight. Involuntarily, note my words, involuntarily his head turns and he finds himself looking at her home, and there she is… drying her hair. Rahul wants to ignore her, but she is waving to him. Signalling him to come. It is a magical moment… and Rahul's determination is not strong enough. How can he leave without meeting her. Rahul's heart lets him down. Before, he can think through the situation, he is walking towards her. All because Sonia waved!

***

'Yesterday, where were you the whole day?,' she is off the block with the first-mover advantage.

'At home, waiting for you.'

'Waiting for me, *Dhut*, you should have come over.'

'So, could you, or you could have sent your brother to let me know I was invited,' Rahul's voice is dripping sarcasm.

'Are you nuts,' it is Rahul's turn to listen, 'Do you think it would look nice, a girl to .. what you said, send message, so soon... and on top of that, I believe you would not have come… there it is.'

'I would have,' he defends.

'Sorry I kept you waiting,' she goes into defensive

'My pleasure,' the sarcasm continues.

Another period of silence follows. Each of them waiting for the other to say something. They realise there is no one to blame, and there is nothing to talk. Both standing at the gate, wanting the time to stop.

She finally breaks the silence, 'When will you be back from college.'

Rahul is cautious, once bitten twice shy. There was nothing much to read in the sentence. 'Five … maybe six,' he tries to sound uninterested

'Can't you come early?'

'Yes, if you want.'

'In this town, I only know you, and with you, I am comfortable,' she sweetens the bait.

'Three O'clock, be at home, I will try.'

'Suits me fine; I will wait.'

She did not give him time to react. Before Rahul could reply, Sonia was walking back to the corridor that would take her to the stairs to her home. Rahul is left stranded at the historical gate where a few nights back he had hurt his fingers. Suddenly, college and friends were no longer interesting enough. Rahul walks with a newfound energy. He is on a mission to get back early.

***

Sonia's image is imprinted in Rahul's mind. She in her wet hair… a bit of water dripping … creating the sensual wet patch near her neck… her squinting as the sun hits her face… the colourful towel trying to hold her damp hair in one place…. Rahul likes it.

***

The over analysing Rahul gets back to thinking and questioning. Was she watching him from the time he stepped out of his house? Was it a mere coincidence that she came out when he was crossing her home? Rahul turns back to look at her home, just in case she is still watching- but there is no one.

Rahul's happiness is bordering on pride. He has finally arrived in life. There is a girl who is waiting for him. A girl who wants him to get back early from college. *Phassi Kudi Phass Gayi*[83]. Rahul is confidence personified. The newfound pleasure of being sought by the opposite gender is plastered all over his face. In a small town like Agra, every small dream and victories are celebrated.

He needs to share it with someone. It can elevate his status – *Aukaat* among peers and friends.

Talking to a female! … she is asking me to meet again! … the nearness… real or perceived are subjects of interest and observation. He needs to be absolutely sure. the news does not travel back to her. Sonia not being a resident of Agra, Rahul does not need to worry.

***

---

[83] The girl has fallen in love.

Rahul usually waits for an empty bus for his 12 Km ride to the college, but today he is in a hurry. He takes the first bus even though it is crowded. He will reach college on time for the first session. Near the college gate, he does not wait for the bus to stop and with rehearsed ease perfectly land in front of Burman dada tea shop, their famed *adda*[84]. Sushant (that is me), his best friend and a day scholar, is already there. We have been together since class 8th, when Rahul's dad was transferred to Agra.

There is no secret between Sushant and Rahul. Sushant is smoking Wills Navy Cut, the brand most student favour. It is a bit costly at Rs 8 for a pack of 10 sticks but is still manageable. The smile on Sushant's face clearly indicates that he too wants to share something. Rahul does not like this pro-position. *Saala* must have met Sneha in the morning. Rahul waves to him, and Sushant acknowledges. Sushant is itching to share developments on his side; however, before he can, Rahul starts.

'Listen, today mark my proxy in the practical class.'

'Do you have some work at home,' Sushant asks innocently.

'Yes, there is this girl, I have to go and meet.'

'Who is she.' Sushant is curious. This is first-hand news for him.

---

[84] A place people meet.

'Subhash Bhai Ke Yaha Aai Hai, Nanital Convent Ki Kanya Hai, Ushne Mujhe Aane Ko Kaha Hai[85]*'*, Rahul blurts out. *'Saale, Jahan Bhi Dekho Who Hi Dikti Hai*[86]*'*. And the picture of the day is her slowly rubbing silken dark curly hair with the pink towel, her eyes fresh and energetic, smiling and saying a lot but silently.

'Is she giving you a line,' Sushant wants to be sure.

'Looks like, I am sure, this time, something will happen.' Rahul tells Sushant with a naughty smile. 'But I have one small problem, please advise me.'

'Bol, Terey Liye Jaan Bhi Hazir Hai[87]*'*

'Should I go and meet her as she wants or should I play hard to get.'

'Don't, you will regret if someone else comes into the picture.' Sushant's advice makes sense. And then Sushant calls for his fee for the advice. *'Chal Aab Issey Baat Par Chai Pila*[88]*'*. Sushant drags Rahul to the tea stall. The free advice is going to cost him five rupees.

***

It is 1:30 P.M., it is the Economics class, a subject Rahul is not interested in. And today, he can think of better things to do with the time. He will meet Sonia's deadline.

---

[85] A girl who has come to Subhash's house and want me to come.
[86] Wherever I look, I only see her.
[87] Ask me, I will even give my life for you.
[88] Now, let's celebrate, pay for my tea.

2:30 P.M., Rahul is at home. After lunch, a quick face wash, he takes a few extra minutes to change. And then hits Sona's home. It is only 3:45 PM.

He knocks and waits, there is no reply.

He knocks harder. There is no reply.

He waits for someone to open the door. Nothing happens.

He places his ears on the door but cannot catch any movement inside. Dejected and feeling cheated, completely frustrated, Rahul walks back.

***

Rahul is super angry. It has now happened twice in a row. Why is Sonia doing this? Is that how one treat their friend? No excuse can explain it. His mind and his heart are having a big fight. The mind wants to evaluate rationally and the heart, wants to give Sonia an opportunity to explain. While he is still undecided, sleep takes over. His tired eyelids cooperate with the tense body, and he is back in the dreamland… there, she is waiting for him.

***

He wakes up at around 5 P.M. His anger is magically replaced by the hunger to meet her. He looks at Sonia's house from the terrace, and as luck would have it, she is there with Sudha; Subhash's landlord's daughter. Sonia and Sudha are walking from one end of the house front to another. They both seem agitated.

What is Sudha doing with her? Has Sonia forgotten she asked me to come back early? Is she waiting for me? Is Sonia expecting me to be on the terrace? If she is waiting for me, she will find a way to get rid of Sudha. Otherwise, she can do whatever she thinks is right.

Rahul waits and keeps watching.

***

Sudha does leave in some time. Rahul compliments himself on reading the situation right. Sonia waves to him. Once again, she is dictating the terms. Rahul, as usual, has no objection to being the puppet of this drama.

***

This is a special day. Rare, but for the third time in the day, Rahul changes clothes. He settles for dark blue denim and a white half-sleeved shirt—time to show some of his toned athletic muscles.

It does not go unnoticed by his mother. She is surprised; her motherly instinct smells the change in her son's life, so she asks her *Rajkumar*[89] his destination. Hearing the answer, she holds back her reaction and informs him that she will be joining them soon at Sonia's house

Rahul is surprised, but like every time, he can do nothing.

---

[89] Prince, here used as the loved one

He does not appreciate this twist in the tale and leaves for Sonia's house.

Sonia is waiting for him at the gate. Rahul is extra careful with the latch this time.

'Hey, dude, where were you today? I have been waiting for you'; Sonia is first to fire. 'Was the class so interesting', not getting a reply she probes further, 'then.'

'I came, but it seems you were sleeping.'

'Why did you not knock', she counters with a smile.

Rahul is shocked. Why should he be the one who is always on the wrong side? Did Rahul not come and knock before leaving? He is sure no one was at home. Or did he sleep in the day and it was part of his dream? Why is Sonia talking like this? It is not as per the script.

Rahul is furious, 'Do you think I will come and not knock on the door… what do you think… am I in play-school… and you the teacher… who needs to guide me for what I must do… you must have been sleeping… that could be the only reason that you did not open the door… I am not sure if you were sleeping…. and how could you not hear me knocking…. come on.'

'Oh, come on, Rahul,' she tries to cool him down.

'Don't you come on me… I missed my class and was here by 15:45 max 1600 Hrs and what do I get… questions and more questions… instead of accepting your fault… all I hear is you blaming me.' Rahul did not want to tell her that he was actually there at 14.45; she would read the desperation in his actions.

Seeing that her effort to control the situation is not helping, Sonia decides to play it differently. 'Did you shout out for me… SONIA SONIA,' she demonstrates. All she gets is an accusing stare. It tells her that Rahul does not find that funny.

'I am sorry', she says. It looks as if she is really sorry.

'Oh, you are, but for what,' It is Rahul's turn to be offensive

'I am the one who called, and then I slept off.

'Get me a good cup of tea, and we shall call it quits'.

'Don't be upset, come in, today I will not only give you tea- but serve you dinner too', she ups the stakes, 'And I will cook'.

***

'I should not have slept.'

'Oh no, I told you I will be a bit late, so it is okay.'

'But, no, I could have left a message with your sister.'

'Come on, what would you have told her? Tell your brother not to come. I will be sleeping. Or tell me what time he really gets back home.'

'No, No, not that Rahul, stop making fun of me.'

***

Rahul can see his mother from a distance, she is on her way to Sonia's house. She is in a hurry. Sonia, too sees Rahul's mother.

'Is your mother going somewhere?'

'No, she is headed here.'

'Oh, yeah, don't bullshit me.'

'I am sure, she told me. But I never thought she would come so early.'

'Come, let's go in,' Sonia suggests.

'Why.'

'Your mother will wonder what we have been up to. It is already 15 minutes since you came, and we are still at the gate.'

'That she must have seen by now. And she would be thinking how to save me from you… *Kala Jadu Kar Diya Tumneh90*'. '*Oh yeah, Nahi Kia Toh Aab Kar Doongi, Chalo Aab Andar91*'. Sonia leads Rahul through the narrow corridor. They walk in a line.

Once inside, they are greeted by Sonia's mother. Silence follows- and it makes Rahul feel a bit awkward. He gets busy with the map searching for unknown countries. Meanwhile, his mother joins them and Rahul is saved from the questioning stares of Sonia's mother.

---

[90] What magic have you done
[91] If I have not put a spell, I will do that now; come inside

Sonia moves to the inside room that doubles as a Kitchen. Taking her cue, Rahul follows after a safe interval.

'Well', he questions her next move.

'Finally, we are alone.'

'Where is your kid brother,' Rahul enquires.

'Cycling somewhere.'

Thank god.'

'For what.'

'For… we are alone…what shall we do now? My mom won't like us to be alone like this.'

'You still mamma's boy', she jokes, but she likes the way Rahul said it.

'Well, my mom will be worried, her son is with a girl like you… alone.'

'What do you mean a girl like you', she questions. Rahul notices her discomfort with a comparative non-contextual statement defining her.

'A beautiful girl like you…'

She blushes and smiles. Oh, how beautiful she is.

Sonia's mother shouts for tea. They get their excuse to remain in the kitchen. Rahul stands next to the door, so that Sonia, her mother and his mother can see him. Brilliant strategic move. It is always good to build trust.

'So, what are your hobbies… Sippy', she asks.

Sippy is a last-minute add-on; there was a pause before she used his nickname… it sounds a lot more intimate and informal… might be that is what she wants.

'Flirting, kissing[92], travelling, Ghazal[93], writing poems and short stories', Rahul tries to sound causal while sharing a long list, at least some hobbies should match.

'You write poems?, she ignores his first attempt at informality.

'Yes, I do… Is writing poems a crime?' Rahul sounds surprised.

'No, No, I mean to be able to write poems, one needs to be emotional to some extent.'

'Don't I look like one', the sparring continues.

'No', the answer comes real fast.

'No! … you do have a right to opinion … You are wrong, and you are right.' Rahul corrects himself in time. 'I am a sentimental fool when it comes to girls.' 'Like you' is unspoken but understood. 'others find me to be a rational person, practical to the T.'

'What kind of poems do you write,' she continues ignoring his

comments.

'Love poems and few that deals with the realities of life.'

---

[92] Truth- Rahul has not kissed anyone to date
[93] A lyric poem with a fixed number of verses and a repeated rhyme, typically on the theme of love, and usually set to music

'Is love not a reality of life.'

'Maybe it is, maybe it is not… who am I to decide what it is.'

'Have you ever been in love?' she casually rolls out the question, and he is not prepared for it… but the situation demands he must answer.

'I think that's a very personal question and too early for me to answer… anyway, in a few days I might say I am deeply in love with you… maybe I am more in love with the idea of love… it seems to happen to me quite frequently… whenever I am with smart, beautiful girls like you.' Rahul winks.

She says nothing. Maybe She did not notice him winking. However, it seemed that her mind was somewhere else.

Rahul points out that the water is boiling and then adds, 'To make tea, you need to add tea leaves.'

'So now you will teach me how to make tea,' she is offended.

'Well, I like tea, and I am particular about it … so if you want, move aside and let me make it.'

She stares hard and continues making tea.

Pouring tea into small cups, Sonia walks into the other room to serve the elderly ladies. Rahul notices the cups are new, and in fact, quite a few things have been added in Subhash's kitchen. Earlier, you could never find two cups of the same design.

He and Sonia take their tea in the kitchen and continue their banter.

***

Rahul observes Sonia. His eyes trace her body.

Sonia is sitting on the *chowki*[94], cross-legged, wearing a tight salwar Kameez that hugs and stretches to her slim frame. Nothing is left to imagine. Rahul can see a hint of a red netted bra under the white top. It makes him a bit uncomfortable. She is immune to it, or maybe she pretends she does not know that he is closely watching her.

Rahul gets up to take some water from the filter, but Sonia holds his hand and signals him to keep sitting. She tells him to stay back for dinner. Rahul jokingly challenges Sonia to get his mother's permission. Sonia is up to the task. She does not hesitate and walks into the other room to calmly informs Rahul's mother that her son will be having dinner with them.

Rahul knows his mother will not like what is happening. But she is left with no choice. As a net result, Rahul stays back. Soon Sonia gets busy cooking, and Rahul resumes tracing her body with his eyes.

***

Rahul and Sonia are still in the kitchen. They discuss a spectrum of topics. She takes the lead, and Rahul does most of the listening. Rahul senses barriers crumbling

---

[94] Very low stool

with every passing minute. One thing leads to another. Soon a stage comes, when they share a few couplets. Each trying to outdo the other … many a time creating new rhyming lines… and then she shares one more couplet.

'Hawa Aaiye Aur Chali Gayi

Hum Sindor Le Kar Bhaitey Raihey

Wo Rakhi Bhand Kar Chali Gayi[95]*

Something snaps. Rahul stares at her. Was it addressed to him? He stops her and blankly tells her, 'Listen … I don't think I can ever have a brotherly feeling towards you… and I don't know if this is a joke, taunt or a threat, and I don't care. But I will treat you like any other friend.'

She does not object. To be honest, she does not react.

The statement leaves a blank unbridged void between them. Rahul is clueless about what to do next, she continues making *chapatis*[96]… as if he was not in the room or that she had not heard his comment.

To hell with her and hell with her games. What Rahul said was a frank, honest confession. And here, *Gori Ladki* is ignoring him. Why can't she just react and tell him what she wants… that is, in case she wants anything.

---

[95] The wind came and the wind went out; I was sitting with sindoor (vermilion that the husband applies on the wife's head as a symbol of marriage), and she tied a Rakhi (a thread that a sister ties on the wrist of brother) to me

[96] A thin pancake of unleavened wholemeal bread cooked on a griddle.

***

Soon it is dinner time. The silence between them is disturbing.

Post meals … it is nearly midnight, and he is ready to leave.

'Give me some of your poems to read,' her tone suggests it is not a request.

'I will think about it.'

'Why,' she probes.

'You know poems are like mirrors. Emotions and feelings are reflected in the poetry. And I don't think I am ready to accept any level of criticism, however good or bad. They are my expressions. And if I do share, once you read them, I will feel naked before you.'

She refuses to react. She stands there in the kitchen staring at him. This time, Rahul decides to stare back. Suddenly she breaks the pregnant pause, 'Will you be back early from college tomorrow.'

'And find you sleeping.'

'No, I will wait for you.'

'Don't give me a second chance to complain…I do have some important classes, and I will bunk for you,' he sugar-coats his threat.

'Ok, then I won't,' she promises.

Sonia looks so innocent. Rahul is sure there will not be a second chance. In many ways, it was his second chance too.

'Bye.'

'Sweet dreams,' and Rahul is not sure if this time it was Sonia who winked.

***

He knew his mother would be waiting for him. She will not sleep before he comes back.

Rahul covers the short distance between the two houses in no time. He looks back and finds Sonia standing at the gate. She has been watching him. Did he still need some proof for her interest in him!

***

At night… Rahul is restless. He keeps replaying the evening, remembering every word and trying to read between the lines to decide if his thinking is right. He tries to match her expressions to statements. Make sense of her smile, the raised eyebrows and other verbal, non-verbal cues. He wants to be sure of her feelings, words and emotions.

Slowly sleep engulfs him with dreams with Sonia in them.

Sadly, in the morning, he will fail to remember any of the dreams.

***

For some stupid reason, the following day, Rahul does not remember what all they talked yesterday. He hardly remember any topic. *Kaala Jadu*[97]. *Gori ladki ka kala Jadu.*

---

[97] Black magic

Rahul is a coiled bundle of energy.
He has some vague notions about things
that I cannot understand.
So cute so shy, pucca husband material,
if not a boyfriend material.
Do, they need to be different? Maybe.
But at least I don't know of a Boyfriend that turned husband!
What rubbish thoughts. Am I having a crush on him?
Or is he just time pass?
Whatever, it does not matter.
He is fun till he decides to act his age.

- Sonia

Challenger

Things are settling down. In just one week, Rahul's schedule has changed. Now his day starts in the second half or whenever the classes finish. The day is defined by his interaction with Sonia. The first part of the day is a torture he must bear to get to the second part. He is no longer interested in studies or friends at their favourite adda.

Rahul attendance in college is below the required 80% even after accounting for the relaxation under the sports quota So, he must attend. At college, He is only interested in knowing when can he leave for home.

***

Today, a few classes have been cancelled, and Rahul is free to go home. It is just 2:00 P.M. Sonia has asked him to come early. And, she promised not to make him wait! It is different; if she wishes him to wait. Rahul can wait till eternity.

But life is a bitch, and things never happen the way we want them.

Rahul reaches home and realises that Sonia, who had asked him to come back early, is not at home. She, her mother and her brother have gone for a movie.! A movie of all the things!! What a let-down. It is worse than getting out at 45 against Jai Hind Colony, missing on what would have been his only 50 of the season. Letting down Bina. Letting down the team that depended on him. And here, Sonia has let him down.

Rahul position in the team is secure. After all, he is the captain. But, today he needs some diversion, and what could be better than cricket.

***

Rahul missed the last few practice sessions. Even if he is the captain, the selection committee and the coach can spring surprises. The anger about Sonia not being at home is a good enough reason for Rahul to report for practice.

At the KhimChand Jain school cricket ground his teammates are surprised to see him. Today, they are using one of the side pitches for practice. Rahul pads up and takes guard.

It is a different Rahul batting today. He is focused and the bowlers bear the brunt of his frustration. They are not bowling at full pace. You don't get selected by getting the captain out. However, it does not make a difference to Rahul, who is relentless in his assault.

The bowlers refuse to take this unnecessary showing off by Rahul. They decide to make a match out of it and go all out. Let's see how good the captain is!

The coach is watching from a distance. He knows his star batsman is in the zone. There is something special today. Only if Rahul can keep this form till the next match on Sunday. He also needs to protect the bowlers from Rahul's relentless, ruthlessly impeccable stroke-play, otherwise they will lose confidence and lack enthusiasm. At the same time, he must protect the batsman without telling the bowlers to slow down.

'Last six,' the coach shouts to Rahul and crosses his fingers. Rahul acknowledges the coach's instructions by raising his tempo and hitting three of the balls for six. Coach is happy his boy is back in form. Rahul is pleased; he is batting well.

If only Sonia could have seen him batting like this.

Rahul's shirt is drenched and it sticks to his toned body. He waves to the bowlers, acknowledging they were really good and joins the coach on the other side of the ground.

Rudra Pratap, the coach, smiles as Rahul packs his kit.

'Rahul, good show, well played; he starts by appreciating his batting.

'Thank you, sir.'

'I liked the way you played Sunil Tandon.'

'What, Sir.'

'Yaar[98] Rahul, Sunil needs some batsman to tell him that he is playable, and you know son, today you did it, keep it up, son.'

'Yes, sir.'

---

[98] Friend.

'And don't miss the practise sessions; team for the league is soon to be announced, you know it.'

'I know sir, but sir.'

'What Rahul, you will now tell me some new excuse, you know I hate excuses.'

'Yes, Sir.'

'But I have been watching you. I can tell when a player is really in the game.'

'Yes Sir.'

'I have seen you play since you were in class 8th. It is easy, in your case. Any problem, son? Studies. Health. *Paisa*[99] *Ya Koi Ladki Ka Mamala hai*[100].'

'No sir, nothing like that, sir.'

'You know Rahul, I can help you in studies, fitness and maybe money, but *Ladki Ka Mamla Alag Hai... woh Problem Hai...* you know, they wipe you out .... they create distances with everything you ever want in life... I hope you know that.' The coach sounds as passionate as Amjad Khan as Jhakaas Anil Kapoor's guru in the movie *Chameli Ki Shaadi*[101].

'Yes, sir, there is nothing like that.'

---

[99] Money.
[100] It got nothing to do with any girl!
[101] A hilarious movie where Anil Kapoor, a budding wrestler committed to the life of celibacy, falls in love with Chameli, the daughter of a coal merchant.

'You know. I know you are not telling the truth. Tell me when you are ready to share. When you feel like it, then come and speak to me. You can count on me. I don't want to lose another player to this Love nonsense.'

'Yes, sir.'

'You know Umesh Nautiyal. He was the perfect first-class player… He played district, zone and then state… captain material… one game in Allahabad… *Saala College Ke Principle Ki Laundiya Pe Fida Ho Gaya… Kuch Zyada Hi Mast… Saala Udney Laga…Pitta102… you know… aur Allahabad Ke Laude Majnu Aur Bhai Ban Gaye… Kneecap Gaya… Aab Langda Hai*[103]… you remind me of him.'

'No sir, really there is no such problem.'

'I hope so for your better future,' Coach pats Rahul on the back.

It is almost 5:30 in the evening when the coach leaves. Was it so visible on Rahul's face that even the coach could read? Rahul is getting worried. In that case, Mom would have definitely seen it … and perhaps even Sonia's mother… that's why she has been staring at him.

Another voice tells him it is not so easy. Maybe the coach was hitting in the dark. It is possible. Anyway,

---

[102] He tried to romance the Allahabad college principal's daughter- he was beaten thoroughly

[103] The guys of Allahabad were like lovers and brothers; they beat him. His kneecap was hit, and now he limps

problem or no problem… it is time to catch up… *Ishq Mai Bhi Six Marrey Toh Manne*[104].

***

Rahul, in addition to missing cricket practice, has been missing the gym too. Today, he played after a long time. The body was opening up and he could feel the muscles revolting with sudden pressure. Rahul takes a quick shower…. and then, instead of rushing to Sonia's house, he simply rests. His tired body needs no encouragement, and soon he is in the dreamland where who else but Sonia is waiting for him.

***

Rahul hears Sonia calling his name. The sound is too loud for a dream. It is like someone was really calling him and that too from near. Rahul's sleep is broken, and as he opens his eyes, there is Sonia standing right next to his bed.

Rahul's reflexes take over. In one single sweeping movement, he pulls the bedsheet over his hairy chest. Next is a T-shirt that he smoothly puts on.

There is silence, and He knows they are alone. *Maa* is at the *kirtan*, sister at her friend's house.

'You sleep too long'. It is a statement and not a question.

'There is hardly anything to do… by the way, how was the movie,' Rahul goes for a counter attack.

---

[104] Hit a six in Romance too, then I will respect you

'Good.'

That's all, nothing about not being at home after asking him to come back early.

'Let's go upstairs,' she suggests.

'Why,' Rahul is still angry.

Instead of answering him, she moves towards the stairs. Rahul follows her.

'Does everything need to have a rational explanation? Does it really need to have a reason?', she challenges.

'As per me, yes… I want to utilise every moment… each moment must help me get nearer to the goal.'

'And what do you gain by being with me,' she is ahead of the curve.

'Not so fast, I do have some plans and reasons for it… it is too early for me to open out to you… and I suffer from fear of failure… so till I am not sure of the success… I am not going to tell you anything… maybe going upstairs with you fits into my plans; this time', Rahul holds her hand and leads the way.

***

Rahul is visibly disturbed by the way things are moving. In the dreamland, it is so easy, he dictates the terms, and she cooperates. But in real life… she knows what she wants… there is too much of 'I' in her. She is demanding and expects everyone to follow her. It makes him uncomfortable.

At terrace, they stand in the area that is lit by the streetlight. The sky is welcoming. Few stars make their presence felt in the dark night.

'Hey… I am told you sing well.' Rahul makes the first call.

'Who told you that?'

'Your mother.'

***

'Will you sing a song for me?'

'I can't… I have a sore throat,' she gives the usual excuse. And in the process acknowledges she sings well enough.

'I won't press', Rahul makes it tough for her to refuse.

'So, what would you like to hear?'

'Well, the songs are, *'Hamey Tum Se Pyaar Kitna*[105]*'* from recently released movie Kudrat or *'Mere Dil Mai Aaj Kya Hai*[106] from Daag or *Jaltey Hai Jiske Liye Tere Aankho Kay Diyey*[107]*'*. Rahul thinks he made her life complicated by limited choices.

'Oh yes, all with names like Rahul, Rajiv, Ramesh like the same kind of songs,' she continues, 'even Sanju likes them.' It was clear that Sonia did not intend to

---

[105] Hindi song titles mean- do you know how much I love you.
[106] Song title from Hindi Film- meaning- do you know what is in my heart today.
[107] Another Hindi film song - meaning- Do you know for who does my eyes sparkle.

share the last name, but it slipped out. She realises her mistake, but it is too late.

'Sanju- who,' It is Rahul's turn to ask the question.

'Oh, Sanju is a close family friend, he is doing Engineering from *Bareilly*… I stay at his place whenever I go there… he too likes poems,' as an afterthought she adds, 'just like you'.

It surprises Rahul, not because of what Sonia is telling him but for the emotions in her eyes. So, who is Rahul, Vacation Stepney, a temporary replacement!

Rahul now has more questions; Does Sonia like him? Does Sonia see Sanju's reflection in him? Or it is like, a boy in every port? Rahul smiles. If that is the case he won't mind being the boy at Agra.

'Are you going to sing or not,' Rahul refocuses on the task. He hates to fight for her attention.

She starts humming the song and then suddenly breaks into it; her voice has a unique tingling effect that suits *'Jaltey Hai Tere Liye'*.

Rahul listens to her carefully. He immerses himself in the experience. And he claps loudly when she finishes. His eyebrows raised in genuine appreciation and it says it all. She is really a good singer. Sonia blushes.

'So, what did you do in the daytime'.

'Household chores, cooking, cleaning, washing… but let me warn you… I am not good at it'.

'You better be', he says without thinking

'Why.'

'Oh! nothing serious… I like perfectionists, who are capable of taking care of the task assigned to them'.

If one was to ask Rahul to repeat and explain it, he would have failed. How should it matter if Sonia was a good cook or not?

***

Sonia and Rahul pick the bedsheet from the clothesline and spread it on the floor. They sit close to each other, bridging the gap with aimless conversation. Rahul is worried, a pause will ruin the experience. Sonia is afraid, a pause may take the discussion into a direction she may not be comfortable with.

It is getting late, and there is no way they can stay any longer on the terrace. Sonia's brother comes searching for her and informs that her mother is calling.

Sonia gets up in a hurry. Rahul notices the hesitation. He understands, Sonia was enjoying the conversation and wanted it to continue; at the same time, she is uncomfortable sitting on the terrace on the dark night alone with him. Rahul does not know of a girl in Agra who could be bold enough like her. He is sure, it is Sonia's convent education that gives her the attitude.

They exchange soft byes, and before he can react, she is gone.

Rahul stands on the terrace. His eyes escorting her shadow till she reaches her home and the door closes on him – from a distance. But, a door is there. If it closes, it also opens.

For a moment I was lost in thoughts
I should not be indulging in.
This guy is a charmer when he warms up to you.
The choice of songs, very romantic.
The mood is a bit dark but fantastically controlled.
I better watch out.
Good, my brother came on time,
not that I doubt or don't trust this guy.

- Sonia

Cheer Up

Rahul bunks college. He was with Sonia the whole day. The two of them just talked, talked and talked. What were they talking? That is a stupid question, Does it matter? What is important is that they were comfortable with each other. Their discussion randomly covered multiple subjects, too fast to register anything. They had lunch and evening tea together and then watched the sun setting somewhere on the western horizon. It was 8:00 P.M. when Sonia left Rahul's home.

***

At about 9:00 P.M., Rahul was trying to fill the void by deep diving into a storyline of a novel, when he heard Sonia call his name. For a moment, he was confused. It was less than an hour since she left, that too after having spent the whole day at his place. And, now she is back. But, who is he to crib and about what. He thanked God for nothing in particular. *Bin Mange Moti Mile Mange Mile Na Bheek*[108.]

Sonia called again. There was no way he could ignore her. She was at his door, all decked up and yes looking

------

[108] You get nothing by begging or you when you want, and when you are not even expecting, you get pearls (read as bountiful)

140

absolutely gorgeous. This time she did not risk rushing into his room unannounced. Fast learner.

Sonia was wearing a pink patchwork *kurta* and a red *churidar* that gripped her legs. A white *dupatta* adding to the allure. A small red pendant dangled dangerously close to her cleavage. The simple silver droplet earring and a mild red lipstick enhanced the impact. Her lips - sensuous.

'Hello, where are you?'

Rahul compliments her, 'You are looking great'.

'Thanks', she says with a smile and Rahul notices that she was blushing.

'What do you want now', Rahul realises his tone was not right.

'Is this the way you talk to a girl?' She is easily offended

'I know it is not the prescribed way.'

'Then you must say sorry.'

'Why the hell should I say sorry when it is you who is disturbing me'. Rahul challenges her.

'Oh, sorry, then I better be moving, I should not be disturbing you'. She turns to leave.

***

Rahul completely misread the situation. He expects she will stop. But in the end, it is Rahul who runs after her. He manages to catch her just before the gate. He is surprised to see her eyes loaded with tears, almost ready to weep. Damn it, how easily she takes offense. And there was nothing much, a silly banter between two young friends.

Rahul feels guilty, and to defuse the situation, he says, 'Won't you like to know what I have been busy with when you decided to surprise me with a sudden appearance?'

'No'. She firmly replies. There is not a hint of emotion in those eyes.

'But I have to tell you, you may like it or not. I was in my dreamland. You don't know how naughty dreams can be, and that's when you interrupted me'.

The frown on her forehead melts, and she asks with complete innocence, 'What were you doing in the dream'. The question presents an opportunity for harmless flirting. This time, Rahul was not going to miss the opportunity.

'Well, in my dream, you and I were in a garden. I was hugging you, and your head was tilted, you were looking at my face, your eyes closed in anticipation, and I was on the verge of giving you the overdue kiss. Should I show you how?'

'No, not now'.

'Not now,' is not 'no'. It is an encouraging sign. It says maybe sometime later. Sonia definitely had the option to rebuke his intentional flirt. But she chose to say, 'Not Now'. Rahul sees that as a welcome sign.

'Will you come with me to the market'. This time the tone is different; she was asking, not dictating.

'Now!!!,' there is a surprise in his voice.

'It is only nine', she counters.

'Only Nine, which country do you live in? People go to sleep, and streets are deserted by this time'.

'That's why I am asking you.'

'Oh, so after all, I do have some functional utility.'

'You want to come with me, or I go alone'. It is both an invitation and a threat.

'Well, then go ahead and ask my mom; that is the only way out'.

'You will never grow up, always mamma's boy', she teases but she is smiling.

'No, I will be escorting a cute girl like you at this hour, nine in the night in Agra, don't you think my mom has something to worry about and that she must know.'

'Ok, baba, there is no way to beat you in arguments. I will check with Aunty.'

Getting permission is no big deal. It is a perfectly valid request. This time, they walk side by side, keeping an expected safe distance as per Agra standards. No words are exchanged. At the market, Rahul takes her to the lane where few shops are still open. Sonia picks up a few cosmetic items, and they start back.

***

Rahul cannot understand the reason for her silence. He is unsure if she is angry or his dream joke has misfired. He stops himself from initiating any conversation. But why can't Sonia tell him? Why should he be guessing?

'Have I offended you in any way', he knows he is venturing into dangerous territory.

'No'. She replies.

'Then why are you quiet? Am I just a bodyguard? For all I care, you could have given me the list and I could have brought them.'

'No, I am just thinking, what all you might be dreaming.'

'Oh, my dreams are naughty enough.' Rahul regrets what he just said. Sonia is blushing, but the good part is that she has not objected. He adds, 'Normally all males just think of sex'.

'Why me', she is inquisitive.

'Oh, don't think it otherwise. There is no rocket science. It is simple. You are a convent educated, and this young man in small-town Agra thinks you could be a fast chick he keeps reading about in the novels'. Rahul continues, 'Definitely, you are frank. You are not like the other Agra girls; I am enjoying this light-hearted harmless banter with you… flirt with you, and that's what I have been doing all the time'. And then Rahul decides to try his luck a bit more. 'As for kissing, if an opportunity comes my way and there is encouragement or no resistance from your side, maybe

I will'. She is visibly shocked, but Rahul is not finished, 'I am confused, I don't know what I want and what I don't.'

She does not react, but he can feel the tension easing. But, Rahul is trapped. He must explain. 'I believe that girls have the power to understand what the boy wants, when they are wooing them. On the other side, boys rarely know what makes a girl smile and what will invite her anger. So, I think the best policy is to be transparent and honest about your thoughts, actions and motives. See what being real gets you. We boys will never understand; the girls will always remain a mystery'. He leaves the thought incomplete and open to interpretations.

'Yes, it's true', surprisingly, Sonia agrees with the observation. Agrees. However, there is a lot left unsaid in that statement.

Rahul drops her home. At the last minute, once again standing at the gate, Sonia asks, and Rahul promises to again return early from college. Latest by 2 PM. This time there is a deadline too.

***

What do you think I did when she asked me to promise?

I Promised. I was more than happy with the invitation.

***

Rahul evaluates his interactions with Sonia. Has there been any change in the way Sonia has been treating him? Has his being readily available made her treat him differently? And then he decides to play hard. He has promised to be back early; he will be back but not at the time she has requested him. He knew it was a risky decision. What happens if he does not come at the time she asked? Will she wait? Will she be angry? How would she react? There were more possibilities than he would have wanted to consider. Each one of them more frightening than the other.

Then there is Bina. He hasn't met her for a long time. She too needs attention., not that she had ever voiced her concern or demanded his attention. However, every time there has been an opportunity, Rahul has made excuses to be with Sonia, who is in Agra for a short time. He knows Bina will fry him alive in case he fails to give her due attention or she comes to know of Sonia. At least Rahul thought so.

***

Clear in his mind... he closes his eyes and sleepwalks into the inviting dreamland.

Such a puppy he is. Talks big. Wants to impress.
But really is open and transparent.
Or is he just checking her out?
Is the conversation she had real?
Or is that all her hyper imagination?
But, whatever, I can see, he respects me, he likes me and I,
that I will leave to time.

- Sonia.

The Odd Day

Luck is never on Rahul's side. Today, for something as silly as a stomach upset, Professor Uttam Adhikari (UA) calls sick. The students know it has more to do with his heavy drinking than eating habits. The last three sessions are cancelled. If only Rahul knew about it earlier, he would have not come to college. He could have spent quality time with his Enchanting Neeli. But then he remembers the decision he had made. To make Sonia wait. Rahul suddenly stops feeling the pressure of promises and deadlines.

As there are no classes, hostellers are the first to leave. Soon it is the turn of day-scholars to leave A few die-hard friends remain with Rahul. Finally, when there is nothing much to do, the gang leaves for the Coffee house, which is in the central part of the city. Rahul will be home by 7:30 P.M.

***

On the way back, Rahul hires a Pedal Rikshaw from the coffee house. His mind is working overtime. He is thinking of the excuses and stories he may have to tell Sonia. What if Sonia has been really waiting for him? Well, she should get the taste of how it feels. What if Sonia retaliates by being unapproachable? Yes, the possibility exists, maybe she will play hardball, but then in some time, she will soften her stand. She will perhaps meet him late tomorrow.

The deed is done. Why worry now? There is no way he could rewind. There was no point worrying about what has happened. The only thing possible is to see how the future is managed. Now, he must willingly accept the consequences and try managing the after-effects to the best of his capabilities.

But what if? This IF is always a big IF.

***

As Rahul opens the gate, he is not ready for the situation. Sonia is prancing like a wounded tigress on the small platform on the first floor. She has been waiting! Sonia wants to know why is he late. As he slowly climbs the stairs, she blocks his way and demands an answer. 'Why are you late? Where have you been?'

Rahul smiles. 'Did I keep you waiting?'

'No, only till three.' She answers. Her look demands an answer.

Rahul is confused. Does it mean, she only waited till three in the afternoon?. Then what could be the reason for her anger? If she gave up after that or got busy with something else, then she should not be angry the way she was.

Sonia and Rahul enter the house together. Rahul picks up a notebook and hands it to Sonia. 'This is my collection of quotes. They may help you cool down.

Meanwhile, I will freshen up'. He had all the time on hand. Keeping her waiting was part of his game plan. While bathing, his hands reach down to the pleasure zone, but he controls himself.

When Rahul joins Sonia, it is time for him to lead the way.

'How is the collection?'

'Nothing much, okayish, just quotes on love, lust and forget me types.'

'Is that a crime?'

'No, not at all, but I expected something better from you.' Getting no reply, Sonia continues, 'I am taking this and will return it after adding a few more quotes'.

'Thanks', that is all Rahul can say.

***

Rahul has a sinking feeling. He is losing the game. Maybe he should do something before the situation becomes unrecoverable and they have crossed the point of no return. The inner voice challenges his sinking feeling. Why are you thinking in these lines? What happened to the confident optimist Rahul?

***

Sonia fires her next question, and Rahul is caught unguarded. 'Do you believe in love?'

Now it is not the easiest of questions to answer. What are you expected to say?

'Let's go upstairs. This is hardly the place to talk about love.' Rahul holds her arm and tries guiding her towards the terrace. Sonia hesitates, not sure about discussing love on the dimly lit terrace. Rahul is hurt, but he understands where she is coming from. She maybe more comfortable in a familiar surroundings. 'Oh, in that case, let's go to your place,' Rahul gives her an option.

They start for her home. Rahul notices, Sonia does not completely trust him. Why did she not go with him? Did she think he will take advantage? Rahul opens the gate of her house and steps in. Sonia turns towards him and, with enhanced confidence without waiting anymore, repeats her question. 'Do you believe in love?'

'Do I believe in love', Rahul repeats the question to buy some time. The answer can define their future status. Why do women always come back to love? But he must answer. 'I do… but it's rare to find love in its true platonic form. There is always a part in any relationship between a girl and a boy, an important part called sex'.

Sonia is surprised by Rahul's answer.

Rahul continues, 'If a boy tells a girl he loves her, I will think he also wants is to sleep with her'.

'Do you love me', Sonia looks at his face.

'No, I desire you'. Rahul clarifies.

'I don't desire you'.

Rahul feels cheated. In a way defeated. Has he lost the game? It is all over?

Meanwhile, Sonia continues, 'But sincerely, I do love you in a very platonic way'. It gives Rahul a fresh lease of life. They smile, laugh and keep talking, fully aware that the conversation is going nowhere. 'You and a compulsive flirt, maybe Agra Romeo number one but still a flirt, you have a long way to go, you don't know anything, Mr. Rahul, you better grow up'.

Even when the statements sounds as if Sonia is treating him like a child and the dice is loaded against him, Rahul is happy. The statement shows that Sonia is not angry with him. However, her mischievous smile worries him. Rahul is not surprised with her next question.

'Today, I saw you with a girl in the city. She must be someone special to keep you back; you promised to return by 2 P.M'.

Oh, now she comes to the real issue. It is turning into an exciting evening. So, Sonia has seen Rahul with someone! The anger was not about his coming late. It was about Rahul being caught with another girl and that the girl could be the reason for him not coming at the appointed hour.. However, Rahul is confused but hides it behind his fake laughter. He has been with his friends all the time. Then, where did this girl come in? A girl who held him back!

***

Truth has many perspectives, and perceptions are always stronger than the reality. Rahul is not aware of any girl, but he is not a fool to let an opportunity like this go waste.

'Where did you see me?'

'Near Bhagwan Talkies.'

'What time.'

'3 P.M.'

Rahul remembers, that Sonia had earlier said that she waited till three. He connects the dots. This is a good time for storytelling.

'What was she wearing?' Rahul decides to play along.

'Blue jeans Pink top.'

Suddenly, everything became clear. Rahul understands the cause of the confusion. Sonia has seen Rahul, while he was waiting for the rickshaw near Bhagwan Talkies bus stand. A beautiful girl in blue jeans and pink top was also standing there, too close to Rahul. Of course, Rahul did not know her, but Sonia also did not know. She assumed that Rahul and the girl wearing the pink top were together. It gave birth to a doubt. Moreover, that was the time Rahul should have been at home with her. Was this a case of pure jealousy? Has it made her angry?

Rahul decides to take advantage of the situation.

'Oh, that girl, her name is Pinky.' Rahul says the first name he can think of. Pink top = Pinky.

Sonia hits him with the book. For the first time, Rahul witnesses the not-so-polite side of her. And then Sonia accuses him. 'Shit, here we planned for a movie and waited for you till two-thirty, even left a message for you …. but when we saw you there…,' she trailed and then said softly, 'I hate you for keeping me waiting.'

'Who's we, and when did we talk about watching a movie'. Rahul is now totally confused.

'Sudha and I thought of it. The movie was a surprise, Dumbo, it's not for nothing that I asked you to come back by 2 PM.'

'That divorcee girl.'

'Yes, that divorcee girl,' Sonia repeated after Rahul. The tone clearly indicating that she did not like the way Rahul said it.

Rahul stopped hearing. His mind was busy conjuring harmless images of him and Sonia in the dark theatre. Having lost the opportunity, Rahul wanted revenge, so, he goes for the kill, 'Oh Pinky too liked the movie, I saw you and pointed you out to her. Poor Pinky She was so insecure seeing you.'

'Really.' It brings a smile to Sonia's face. 'You should have introduced us.' Sonia is yet not finished, 'I hate you for not telling me and I have to get a confession out of you, but I still hate you for not keeping your promise.'

'Are you crazy? You were quite a few rows in front, and do you expect me to shout inside a theatre?

Stupid… I did think of telling you, but you never gave me a chance… and as I have kept you waiting… I was not sure how to tell you.'

Sonia gets up, and Rahul holds her wrist, telling her to sit down. She is in no mood to follow his advice. Rahul pleads with his eyes and touches his ears to say he is extremely sorry. Sonia smiles.

***

Unpredictable Sonia wants to go for a walk. She has no destination in mind. Knowing the town and the time it is Rahul is worried. Sonia tries telling Rahul something, and he does not get it. Was she talking about making him repent his actions? Was she threatening? Rahul is tensed and he involuntarily recites Hanuman Chalisa109.

"Bhoot Pishaach Nikat nahi aavey, Mahavir jab naam sunavey. Nasey rog hare saab peera, japat nirantar hanumat bira, sankat te hanuman

chudhavey, man kram vachan dhyan joh lavey[110]*"*

Rahul knows, the walk is an excuse. There is something more sinister in her mind. There has to be a hidden agenda. There is nothing in his control. He has no option but to play along.

---

[109] Hanuman Chalisa is 40 verses in honour of the son of the wind - monkey-faced god- Hanuman. Hindus believe that reciting Hanuman Chalisa ensures nothing wrong happens to you. It takes care of ill things around you and protects from any harm.
[110] Lines from Hanuman Chalisa, that involuntarily gets in lines of the followers when they are faced with issues that seems out of control.

She takes time to get ready. But when she steps out, it is worth the wait. Seeing the almost jaw-dropping expression of Rahul; Sonia smiles. She knows she is beautiful, and right now, she is jaw dropping wow in a red sleeveless top, a short black skirt and a matching pair of high heels.

Both the dress Sonia is wearing and the time is very late by Agra standard. It is not safe. If that was not enough, at this hour madam has decided to wear a short black skirt.

"Mahavir Vikram Bajrangi, Kumati Niwar sumiti ke sanghi[111]"

Rahul is wearing his regular faded Demin and a loose shirt. Changing clothes will be inviting his mother's rapid-fire questions. Where are you going? When will you be back? Who is with you? Is this time for a walk? Can't you do this in the morning? And most likely, the walk will be abandoned.

"Sankat Kate Mite saab peera, joh sumirey Hanumat Balbira[112]"

And with that, Rahul is finally ready for the walk.

***

Sonia promises it will be a short walk, maybe till Noor Bano Garden and definitely not beyond it. Rahul is still

---

[111] Line from Hanuman Chalisa meaning- powerful lord Hanuman who removes bad thoughts and brings in good thoughts.
[112] Another line from Hanuman Chalisa, that says just chant the name of Hnumaanjee and everything will be fine.

uncomfortable with the thought. It is after all Agra. A beautiful girl in a sleeveless top and a very short skirt by Agra standards walking in its dim-lit roads is definitely calling for trouble.

The area where Rahul and his family live is considered safe. But why take chances? Every area has its own set of rowdies. All Rahul wants is to drop her back in the safety of her home. However, Sonia has some other ideas and she is totally comfortable with the situation.

'So, what's your zodiac sign.' Rahul asks to distract himself from his worries.

'Guess.'

"Scorpio.'

'Right, but how did you guess.'

'Oh simple, they say, one gets used to a Scorpio's bite.'

'When did I bite you,' she asks playfully.

'Well, that's what you have been doing all this time.'

***

Rahul and Sonia find themselves in a dimly lit stretch of the road. A few local boys are sitting on their bikes. Rahul knows them by face. They are safe types. However, he has other ideas to take advantage of the situation.

Rahul starts walking closer to Sonia. Slowly but confidently, he holds Sonia firmly by the waist.

'Don't.' She almost shouts with visible irritation in her voice.

'Don't what.'

'You know, what I mean, don't place your hand like that.'

'If you wish.' Rahul is dejected. One can make out from his voice that he neither expected nor did he like her asking him to remove the hand. Rahul is a born actor, and for him, the act is not yet over. He signals her to be quiet and continues holding her by the waist. When they finally reach a well-lit part of the road from where they can see the house, he removes his hand. And then shares with Sonia his reason for holding her the way he did. 'You saw those boys... *Woh Eis chowk Ke Lafange Hai*[113]... and would you know why you have not been whistled at, even when you are dressed like this?'

She raises her eyebrows as if saying, you tell.

'Because Miss Sonia, I had my arms around you... it is a way to tell them you are with me. And that they better not try anything silly.'

'Thanks.' Rahul knows this time she meant it.

Walking side by side, slowly and with much hesitation Sonia's hand finds Rahul's hand. Soon the fingers are interlocked. They sense a different warmth radiating from their clasped palms.

---

[113] Harmful elements of this area

As they reach nearer home, they unlock their fingers and involuntarily a decent distance creeps between them. The status is changed, did it change some time back? However, there is a new sense of belongingness and feelings.

"Bhudhiheen Tanu Janike, Sumiro Pawan Kumar. Bal Budhi Vidhya Dehu Mohi, Harhu Kalesh Bikar[114]"

***

Are they now more than mere friends? Has Sonia developed a soft corner for him? Maybe. A simple step… maybe this is an innocent pause in their lives. But for Rahul, this moment is a fountain of unanswered questions. More questions than he can answer.

"Yes Kya Hua, Kaise Hua, Kab Hua, Kyon Hua, Jab Hua, Tab Hua, Chodho yeh na soocho"

The Bollywood number came to his mind and he started humming it. What happened, how did it happen, when did it happen, why did it happen, whatever happened, whenever it happened, stop thinking about it, go with the flow.

***

They part with a promise to meet again. There were a lot many unsaid promises being made. Life is all about fixing coordinates, aligning and synchronising, giving

---

[114] From Hanuman Chalisa- meaning- I remember you lord Hanumanj, give me power, intellect and education and remove all obstacles in my way.

and taking, happiness and sorrow. The only duality survives on this planet earth, including life and death, the two most significant truths of life. In between everything else is a probability and a possibility. And Rahul wanted just to be certain about some of the possibilities.

I don't know what happened,
when did my hand find itself in his hands
and when did our fingers interlocked.
Yes, I was angry with him,
but don't know the cause of it.
Was I jealous? NO, why should I be?
There have been no commitment
and no we have our own lives.
But, seriously while we held hands, It felt great,
I could have kissed him… but then…

- Sonia

Favourable

Life is like a game of chess but far more complex. No one ever lost or won in it. No one holds an advantage for long. The results are too distant to be visualised. To make a game out of it, requires strategic intervention.

Rahul's day starts with good news. The University is closed until further notice. The tension between two student lobbies culminated into a major fight where few were seriously injured. The Vice-Chancellor and Dean have taken the easy way out. Close the campus, and vacate the hostels. It means Rahul now has a legitimate reason to be at home and that means to be with Sonia. No proxy to be marked. However, his mother's anxiety levels is sure to go up.

Rahul shares the news with Sonia. Now, only social expectations and family reactions control the amount of time they can spend together. They rediscover subjects to discuss. Indeed, they repeat many without being aware of it. And definitely without letting the other party know of it. It does not matter. No one is complaining. They discover common interests. Their situation is like milk on the stove; it is simmering with coiled eagerness to do more than just talk.

***

Cricket is Rahul's favourite sport. However, he is decently good with most of the games. For some time Sonia has been pestering him to teach her at least one game. Rahul considers exposing her to Chess. Sonia gives him a chance for an honourable escape. She tells him, it is okay, there is no pressure. However, her saying it makes Rahul happy and more determined to teach her. Rahul is a bit disappointed, Sonia has shown no interest in a contact sport. Otherwise, he was ready to be the Viru of his Basanti[115]. Finally, the stage is set. A new Chess Board is purchased from Bholanath Sports.

***

The training starts as soon as the chessboard arrives. Rahul explains the basics. However, there is a twist in the tale. Ajay, Sonia's brother, is super excited to see the chessboard. Sonia teases him that finally she has found someone to teach her chess. And then she breaks the news that Rahul is going to help her play chess.

'Oh, is that so'. Ajay is surprised.

'Yes, I think I am a decent player'. Rahul speaks with confidence.

'Well, let's have a game then,' Ajay throws him a challenge.

'Yes, why not,' Sonia pushes for it.

---

[115] Viru, played by Dharmendra and Basanti by Hema Malini, are two characters in the super hit film Sholay. In one of the scenes, Viru teaches Basanti how to shoot.

There is no way Rahul can now refuse the challenge. If he is teaching Sonia, then he must demonstrate his expertise by beating her little brother in the game. The match is on.

The board is set and Ajay moves his Pawn. It is then that Sonia shares the secret, and Rahul's confidence Is punctured. Ajay, is an under-14 District level player. Ajay is too good for rusty Rahul, and Rahul loses faster than he can say, Bishop or Knight.

Rahul cannot face further humiliation. He tried his best. He concentrates on the game to save his skin. The next set of moves are brilliant and Ajay too is impressed. But when Rahul was busy saving the Queen, Ajay moves from the flank and sets up a checkmate.

Rahul's king is helplessly surrounded by two Knights, and the Queen is guarding the lone corridor the king could have taken to escape. Even Sonia can read his impending defeat.

Rahul realises that Sonia's excitement with chess is the reflection of her desire to defeat the male in the family in the game he excels. Rahul has completely let her down.

'Ajay, you play so well; why don't you teach your sister the basics and then I will take over'. The fragile male ego takes over, and even after losing, Rahul is unwilling to surrender.

'Chess needs brains, and girls don't have them'.

'Oh', is all Rahul can say.

'Okay, I am bored, what can we do? This chess is so technical,' Sonia comes to Rahul's rescue.

'There is enough in and around the city, many historical places. But one needs to find time for it'.

'I will, I like that', Sonia continues, 'and will you show me around?'

There is a pause. Rahul has a tough time controlling his excitement.

'Yes', it is the obvious answer. Rahul nods to her.

Another cup of tea is served, and the plan to visit the famous Raja Garden takes shape. Unfortunately, the list of people going to Raja Garden includes Sudha and Ajay. It is up to him to make the best of it.

***

Raja Garden is at the heart of the city, some 3-4 Km from Rahul's home. Locals know the way through the maze of interconnected lanes and back alleys. They don't depend on the unpredictable local transport buses. Walking through the crowded streets is the fastest way to reach Raja Garden. The social norms of orthodox Agra with a dominant Muslim population requires that they keep a safe distance between them… holding hands is unthinkable.

***

Raja Garden is designed with concentric circles and defined quadrants. The outermost ring is for walking. The north quadrant has food courts, the south quadrant in the middle ring has rides and swings. The central area is dedicated to a warrior statue. East quadrant is the knowledge sector with space for meditation and benches for relaxation; it is different that most of the garden is used by young couples for totally different activities. On the Western side is the greenest part with a small pond in its centre.

After buying the entry tokens, they all move in. Sudha and Ajay hit for the south quadrant for the swings. Sonia and Rahul slow down. Rahul guides Sonia to a secluded area on the western quadrant. There is a much smaller pond. At the centre of the pond is a small concrete island that can only be reached using a wrought iron bridge. The narrow bridge is painted in bright colours, and the area is dimly lit. Here Rahul plans to find some quality time with Sonia.

Sonia says nothing while Rahul manoeuvres her away from Sudha and Ajay. It surprises and confuses Rahul. Sonia could have insisted that they all remain together, but she chooses not to do so. When Rahul and Sonia reach their destination, Rahul is happy to notice they are the only couple there. Rahul and Sonia sit facing the bridge, and Rahul looks into Sonia's dreamy eyes. His confidence grows. Just when he has built the courage to be a wee bit more adventurous, tragedy strikes.

A Hawaldar[116] appears and challenges them. 'Hey, what you are doing here.'

---

[116] A lower ranked policeman- the beat constable.

'Nothing', This is a new situation for Rahul.

'Who is this, girl?'

'Friend.'

'If she is a friend, what you are doing here'. The Hawaldar knows the territory and is getting into his act.

'Why it's a garden, and we are sitting here.'

'Garden, and how come you have only found this dark place... saala badmash[117].'

'No Hawaldar Saab. We are with other people, she is a guest at our home, and I am showing her around.'

'Do you think I am mad... I understand your type of boys and her kind of girls... *Saale Poorey Garden Mai Yeh Hi Andheri Jagah Mili Dikhane ko... Jhoola Nahi Mila... Aquarium Nahi Mila... Woh Museum Nahi Mila... harami*[118].'

'Saab, don't say anything more.'

'Is she your sister?'

'No.'

'Then', Hawaldar is in no mood to give up on a possible chance to make some money.

'Then what.'

'Shall I take you to lock-up', Hawaldar presses for the kill.

---

[117] Rascal.

[118] In the whole Garden, you found only this place that is not lit. You did not find the swings, aquarium, museum

'Saab, leave it.'

'Why.'

'Because Police In-charge Sub Inspector Radhey Shyamjee is a family friend.' Rahul adds, not that he will ever think of getting Radhey Shyamjee involved in this.

'Oh, so you should have told me so.' Hawaldar stance changes. 'See *baba*, the garden closes by 7:30, and it's not really safe for girls, this area, you know, you should leave.'

'So, you should have said.' Rahul jokes with him and signals Sonia to leave.

Sonia is at a distance and not privy to the conversation. She wants to know why they are leaving so early.

"I like it here; it is so quiet', Sonia tells Rahul.

'Let's just leave.'

'But why.'

'You will not understand.'

'Try me.' Sonia is not easy to convince.

'Oh, so have it your way.' Rahul hates to be questioned. 'You want to know what Hawaldar said, well, let me tell you. He said, this Garden in the evening is a pick-up joint, where women find their customers. As we seem to be from a good family, we should leave this place before someone mistakes you as a call girl and me as a pimp. Anyway, the Garden closes at 8 P.M.'

Then he added almost in whispers that only Sonia could hear, 'Happy now' to show his irritation.

The moment Rahul finished, he knew there were better ways to tackle the situation. He could see Sonia was offended. Within few seconds, their status changed from 'Happy with each other' to 'Don't know why I am here' to 'We don't know each other.'

They walk back like strangers. Sudha senses something is wrong. Her arched eyebrow seeks an explanation, but Rahul simply shrugs.

Halfway through to home is the *Kelwa Mata Mandir*[119]. A temple with a huge local following.

Rahul takes the puja thali from the shop. It has the usual items, flowers and Prasad. He expects that Sonia will join him but nothing like that happens. By the time he completes the *Parikrama*, Rahul is sulking and he is not sure why Sonia is sulking. What wrong has he done. She wanted an explanation to the incident and he provided her just that. Nothing more or nothing less. If you want to know then be willing to hear the answer. The answer anyway was generalised and there was nothing personal about it. He has been straight and honest. He only told her because she insisted.

The day started with a promise of gaiety and fun has turned into one of the worst days for Rahul. Sonia is not in her elements. And she refuses to see merit in

---

[119] A local temple dedicated to Goddess Kelwa.

whatever Rahul does. Sonia's mind is somewhere else. She is thinking… and Rahul is worried about what she is thinking.

***

Just before they hit the home stretch, the last 200 meters from the final destination, her mood changes. There is a perceptible change. To date, Rahul fails to understand what happened that evening.

She stops at a multi-utility shop and buys 2 bubble gums. She offers Rahul one. Rahul refuses to take anything from her.

'Why are you angry with me', she asks.

'Yes, I am, so what.' Rahul is not willing to give in easily.

'Are you angry because of the way I behaved?' She probes.

'Yes and No, well, yes I am bugged by your mood swings, and No, you have all the right to behave the way you want.' Rahul is brutally honest with her.

'Sorry.'

'For what.'

'For being like that', she explains.

'You and your mood; you can do whatever you want; who am I to say anything?'

'Don't talk like that.'

'No, I will say because that is the truth.'

She holds his hand and looks into his eyes. Rahul can see her innocent eyes pleading. It is difficult for him to continue with the sensitive sulking act.

'Well, what is lost is lost,' he says to gain the upper hand. 'Till date, you have only seen the loving and caring side of me, just wish you never see the other side of me.' It is a harmless threat, and Rahul knows it. He will constantly adjust and adapt to Sonia's likes and dislikes. He can't be rude to her for long.

***

They reach the intersection, where they must part ways. This time there is no customary goodbyes- just a glance that says- tomorrow will be another day- and we will meet again.

How adorable Rahul is. How caring he is.
Definitely he likes me.
Maybe he loves me and is too shy to say.
Maybe he does not know how to say so.
I have thought enough and I must confess, I like the guy.
I again felt so much warmth and
a shiver that ran through me
when I held his hand for that fraction of a second.
In the coming days, I will try to probe where we stand.

- Sonia

Lost Day

Subhash works in shifts and gets a compensatory day off when the shift changes. Today, he is going to be home throughout the day. If that is not enough, he decides to play the perfect Mamujaan[120] and decides to take his sister's family for an outing.

Sonia does not ask Rahul to join. Maybe it is just a family thing.

***

An empty mind is a devil's workshop.

With no explanation for Sonia's behaviour, Rahul worries.

What if Sonia never talks to him? What if she is that stubborn?

Rahul wants to know what his crime is? Why is he being punished?

He is sure that it is not about refusing bubble gum!

Rahul feels cheated.

He is annoyed and questions, What does Sonia think of herself?

---

[120] Maternal Uncle.

Fair skin. *Gori Ladki Hogi Apnea Ghar Mai*[121].

Is she the only one who has the right to be sensitive? What about me?

Aapna Bhi Toh Kuch Haq hai[122].

---

[121] How do I care, if she is fair and beautiful.
[122] I, too, have some rights.

I would have wanted Rahul on this family trip.
But I could not be the first one to suggest that.
No one else did. No one felt the need.
There were four of us,
and two Rikshaws were comfortable for us.
If Rahul was to join,
he would have been alone in another Rikshaw,
but we would have been together. lost time,
I have not been able to talk to him.
He was so grumpy yesterday
that he won't accept the bubble gum.
Well, let us see-how things move.

- Sonia

Smoke & Fire

Time has the answer to everything, and time finds ways to adjust and resolve differences. Rahul's case is no different. The hunger to meet Sonia is stronger than the anger for not being invited for the outing, and it is that simple.

***

Rahul wants to make up for the lost time. Sonia would soon be going back. And Rahul is still acting like a kid. *Begani Shaadi Mai Abdulla Deewana*[123].

Rahul decides it is time for him to get some time with her. With a plan in his mind and spring in his steps, Rahul lands at Sonia's home early in the morning. He has a decent plan and proposal. He asks Sonia if she would want to join him for *'Guns of Navarone'* playing in the morning show at Gold Cinema. Very few theatres in Agra screen English movies, and the ones that do, do it as special morning shows during the weekend.

Sonia quickly agrees to the plan. Her mother grants them permission. No questions asked.

---

[123] Getting too involved in things that do not concern you.

It seems like last night's trip to Raja Garden and the Bubble-gum episode never happened. Rahul pinches himself to check if he is not dreaming. This was too simple. He is on cloud nine when Sonia breaks his bubble. She plans to take her brother to the movie.

All this while, Rahul has been thinking of the corner seats in the darker end of the hall… the last row, to be precise. No, Sonia has not given him any hint of her interest in Rahul, and it was silly for Rahul to think he could take liberties he takes in his dreams. But, liberties or no liberties, corner seats or not, taking her brother for the movie is a complete spoiler for the situation.

Fortunately, Ajay is more interested in a tennis ball cricket match in the neighbourhood and refuses the invitation. Rahul is saved from the situation. However, it is a temporary respite. Sonia's mother changes her mind! Now they are no longer going to the movie, there is some work at home, and Sonia needs to help her mother.

Rahul is back at his home, *'Laut Ke Budhu Ghar Ko Aayeh*[124].' Why does it always happen to him?

***

It is afternoon when Rahul revisits her. He finds Sonia uncomfortable in his presence. He thinks it may be her period. He has no way of knowing unless Sonia tells him, which he knows she won't.

---

[124] A fool returns home at the end of the day.

In our society, males of the house are blind, dumb and mute when it comes to periods. They won't have any idea. Most likely, the husbands don't even know about wives' chums unless they are denied sex.

No, progressive Rahul is not paranoid about periods. It is a natural thing to happen. But like any other girl, Sonia may be uncomfortable, and Rahul can do nothing about it. Absolutely Nothing. And he may never know if his reading of the situation is right or wrong.

***

At 4P.M, Sonia serves tea and guides Rahul to the staircase. They are halfway up to the terrace when she stops, pulls out a cigarette, and lights it with practised ease, taking a long first drag. This is an unexpected act that catches Rahul unaware. He is momentarily speechless.

'You smoke,' he asks. The tone says it all.

The question is natural and involuntary.

In small towns like Agra, ladies are not expected to smoke. And if they do, they don't do that publicly.

'Well, you can see, can't you?'

Rahul has no reply.

'Don't know… why you guys think girls can't smoke, and anyway, I smoke for fun and not as a habit.'

Rahul keeps quiet.

'I know Rahul, I am a bad girl, and I know you were itching to hit me for smoking.' Rahul does not contradict her assumption. 'There are many things about me you don't know,' she looks intensely at the tip of her stick, 'Many,' she adds as an afterthought.

This is a god-sent opportunity for Rahul. It can go either way. But he will know only if he acts. The timing and the location could not have been better. On impulse, Rahul takes the cigarette and throws it out.

'So, happy now.' Sonia says.

'Yes, I am; there is something that women must not try doing.'

'There is nothing that a girl can't do.'

'Well, don't be too sure about it; this is not the place or the time. Otherwise, I would have shown you what a guy can do and a girl can't. A lot of naughty images flash in Rahul's mind.

Sonia stares at Rahul, and a tiny tear rolls down. Rahul takes out his cigarette pack, lights one and gives it to her.

'Trust me, this is the last time you are smoking before me.' Rahul says it with fake authority and is pleased to see that Sonia does not take offence to his statement.

'Yes.'

'Are you leaving smoking for me or just because I asked you?'

'Might be, but surely you won't see me smoking,' she promises.

Rahul wipes the tears that are threatening to wet her rosy cheeks. He tells Sonia to wash her face. No way he can put his reputation at stake. What if someone sees her weeping? What will they think?

Sonia is back from the washroom. She feels rejuvenated and fresh. She smiles, and it makes Rahul feels a lot better.

***

It is almost dark, and they have been chatting on the staircase for a long time. Sonia leads Rahul to the terrace. It is deserted and very dimly lit. There are a few unused boxes, a bedsheet spread on the wire for drying, and another bedsheet with cut pieces of mango kept for drying. A small cot is resting against the wall. Rahul pulls the cot and makes himself comfortable. Sonia sits at some distance and is busy searching for something in the sky above.

They have been silent for some time.

Rahul thinks Sonia wants him. You can't get a clearer signal from a girl. He definitely desires her. But the deafening silence between them tells him to proceed cautiously and resist the temptation to hug her.

Rahul hardly has any experience with love and sex, and his education is restricted to boy chats and porn movies. The half-baked knowledge passed by senior students and Indian films providing the study material.

Playboy and Debonair have been the default visual references.

Rahul is totally unsure of their relationship. He wants to tenderly and passionately kiss Sonia, … but courage fails him again.

***

So, Rahul takes on a philosopher role and addresses one more question to Sonia.

'Do you know why I want to be alone with you? Because I want you to know certain facts about life? You may think I am a male chauvinist? Well, just to make it clear, I am not. Irrespective of you or me desiring, there will always be jobs that only men can do… like there will be a few, which only women will know how to do best.'

She keeps to herself. Rahul continues, 'Do you know why women are called the fairer sex.'

'No.'

'As from their childhood, they are taught to be fragile, polite to be correct, leave all manual and labour-intensive work for the man to do… there is always logic in things coming from time immemorial.'

'Like.'

'Why should the wife's height be less than the husband's?'

'Why.'

'By being at eye level, she is respectable and is not looked down. Her shoulders are where her husband's heart is so she can understand him better. The man protects her but takes emotional support from her.' Rahul surprises himself at the ease with which he could reel off the answer.

***

'Now, if you want to read the poems, come and collect them. I think you will understand and appreciate them. Offering Sonia the opportunity when she was least expecting it was Rahul's way of doing damage control.

***

Nothing much happened that night. They needed to bridge substantial mental and emotional gaps before attempting anything adventurous.

It is very late, around 1030 P.M. when Rahul finally leaves.

Sonia is adamant about getting the book now. So she walks with Rahul and waits at the gate. He brings the book and walks Sonia home.

***

As per Rahul, the day had ended on a good note. At least it was a lot different than yesterday when he was worried that he had gone too far. As he enters the land of dreams and fantasies, he knows she will be waiting for him.

Silly guy this Rahul is!
I cannot be more direct
about me wanting to have my first kiss.
But, then I do expect him to take the initiative.
What is he waiting for an invitation card
with date-time-venue for the kiss?
There are a few days left on my trip to Agra.
Still, I am not sure of myself. Not sure if we will meet again.
Maybe the best way to learn about life. Maybe…

- Sonia

Immature Class

Rahul's sister is younger to him. And so, it is usually he who runs household errands. Everything from slipper repair to biscuits for the guest or the monthly groceries is his area of operations.

Today, when he was returning from the market after buying curd, he crossed Sonia on the staircase. She was returning from his house. The staircase is a narrow one. Two adults can't cross each other without some contact, it is Sonia who flattens herself against the wall allowing Rahul space to move up. It looked as if she did not want Rahul to touch her, a clear sign that she was angry.

'Come up,' Rahul suggests.

'No.'

'You seem to be angry, any problem.'

Sonia says nothing. Her eyes show that she is furious.

'Sonia, what's this time.'

Rahul is irritated. If she is angry, she should tell.

'So, have it your way, I thought you should be the first to hear some good news, but it seems it is not important for you.' Rahul's voice takes a higher pitch. It is time for him to throw the bait and use his persuasive skills, 'I will share, if you retrace your steps and come back.' Sonia follows silently. As soon as they are in, she cannot hold herself, 'so tell me what cannot wait.'

"Well, you tell me first, why you are behaving like *Kali*[125] today."

'I have every reason to be angry', she whispers as if Rahul should know the reason.

'How will I know, unless her highness, the queen of hearts, Sonia, the great shares with me.'

'What do you guys think, who gives you the right to classify girls, branding them?'

'Oh, so you have been reading the article on the classification of girls and it is bothering you.'

'Yes.'

Shit, Rahul is now in a no man's land. The notebook he gave Sonia had a small section on how to classify girls.

'Do you girls classify boys?' Rahul counters.

'Yes, we do,' at least she was honest.

'So, the boys too do the same, they classify girls, simple enough. I see no harm, and anyway, the article is a way of putting forward my views on the subject.'

---

[125] One of the furious and angry avatars of Goddess Shakti

'I just want to know in which category you place me.' Rahul realises the real issue.

'You may not like what I tell you', Rahul is on guard. He knows, anything he says will be held against him, if not now, then sometime in the future.

'We shall know.' She sidesteps the statement.

'You will not interrupt me… till the time I finish and tell you to speak.'

'Ok.'

***

It is time for Rahul to make his most important speech. To choose the words and watch for her reaction and uses them as his guide through his unplanned monologue.

***

'As far as I know, we form our opinion based on impressions, expectations and past experiences. These impressions get loaded into our memory system, and we create stereotypes. Hell, we don't even wait to meet the person; we start making a mental sketch and slot them even if we only hear about them. What you read is merely a simplification of the stereotype from a growing teenager's perspective.'

'All the girls can be classified into three simple types.'

'First are the City Tarts. Leave them alone. They cause problems. They give you more pain than pleasure. They are independent and isolated; they do not belong to anyone. For them, what matters is them. They have shallow loyalty. They will do everything and anything to be successful. They are flashy and adventurous. They hate being on the losing side. In case of a crisis, if they are forced to make a choice, they will dump you before you can say D.'

'Second; the Beauty tease. These girls are beautiful externally with a suspect moral compass. They are good for satisfying the physical hunger six fingers below the belly button. They are easy to get and manage. They will willingly live in the shadow of someone else's success if it suits their purpose. They are temptresses with an insatiable physical hunger. And enjoy the power they gain by using feline charm.'

"The third category is the one with solid character, inner and most likely external beauty. They have their cultural values intact. They respect societal norms and regulations. Friendship with them is highly protective and productive. They value relationships. They are life-partner material. Unfortunately, it is tough to locate and identify them. They do not easily mix up with boys. For them every boy is a suspect.' Rahul pauses for a breather.

'So, in which category do you place me,' She throws a direct question.

'I have not finished, so you can't ask me anything, hold on to your question.' Rahul buys time to avoid collateral damage. And then continues, 'But these impressions are dynamic, they change with time, expectation, experiences, age and maturity. You interact with people, and every interaction places the prior understanding for re-examination. In the process you re-evaluate. The experience may end up in strengthening or weakening the perception or create a new perception.' He was nicely covering his track, 'What do you think, which category would I have bracketed you? As you are angry, you most likely think I place you in a category you don't want to be placed in. So, should this anger then not be directed inwards.'

'Rahul, we are talking about your impressions of me, so you answer the question.'

'Well, I place you in the third category.' Rahul could see her smile start, then he added, 'but.'

'But.'

'You are at the edge of the third group.'

She reacts as expected. 'You are telling me you can't decide if I belong to the second or the third category! She is angry, 'Do I look like the kind of girl who is of loose morals and will allow someone to exploit me.' Sonia is losing her composure.

'No.'

'Then.'

'I am not sure, if I should place you in the third or the fourth category?'

'You never mentioned a fourth category,' she complains.

'How can I tell you about the fourth category. the notebook you read is old … with age, I have re-defined my outlook… then I met you a few weeks back, that is when the idea of a possibility, of the fourth category took shape.' Rahul continues, 'They are beautiful with strong character and a positive aura around them. Most guys will think twice before approaching them.'

It has the expected effect. Every girl likes to hear such compliments. Sonia's was no different. Sonia smiles and Rahul thinks he can relax. There is a flame of surprise in her lovely blue eyes. The wild untapped fire wanting to be tamed. Her lips hinting at some caged passion. It is then that Sonia remembers Rahul was talking about some good news.

***

'So what is the good news.' Sonia finally asks.

'I am now available 24 hours a day.' Rahul tries sounding casual.

'Are you joking, or you serious,' she does not believe him. 'What about your college and classes.'

'All closed till further notice.'

She seeks no explanation. She does not even ask the reason as to why college is closed.

'Then come over to my place by 4.30,' Sonia extends an impromptu invitation.

'No, I can't.'

'Why not.'

'I am going to sleep now and will meet you at seven,' Rahul makes an attempt to take charge.

'Let's compromise, what about six.' she is negotiating.

'All right,' Rahul did not want to risk his luck.

'You are really too cute,' saying this she plants a hurried kiss on Rahul's cheeks and leaves a perplexed Rahul in the room. He wonders, what was that in aid of?

***

Words cannot express Rahul's feelings at that moment. A tingling sensation started at his head and weaved its way down to the toes. It was pure bliss. Think of it, the girl he has been chasing just kissed him. It was an impromptu action. Why? How does it matter? Things were definitely picking up. *Bin Mange Moti Miley Mange Mile Na Bheek*[126].

***

The kiss gave him a different type of confidence and comfort. He was excited and at peace at the same time. Once he slept, he woke up at 8 P.M and this time he did not remember the dream.

***

'I am sorry, I am late,' Rahul apologises for the impact. The kiss that he got in the afternoon demanded him to

---

[126] You may get a pearl when you are not asking for it and may not get alms when you seek them.

play the role of a perfect gentleman. And, if saying sorry can make things better, what is the harm in doing so?

'Waiting increases the pleasure of meeting,' she says with a wicked look in her eyes and adds, 'I am sorry too.'

'For what.'

'For acting the way I did for last few times.'

'When,' Rahul fakes a surprise. He knew what she was hinting at. 'Forget it,' that is the only reaction he has.

***

'Let's move to the terrace,' Rahul invites Sonia.

'Why.'

'Well, I do plan to ask you something, and this is not the right place.'

'Then lead', she starts moving.

This time, it is Rahul who leads the way.

***

The cot is resting against the wall. So, someone has repositioned it. Rahul takes the cot and places it properly. He is careful not to make noise. There was no point in announcing to the whole world, here they are.

She sits on the cot, with her knees tucked in, and her back is resting on the wall.

Rahul hesitates for a moment unsure where to sit. Should the preferred social distancing of Agra be followed? To hell with it. He finally lies down with his head comfortably resting on Sonia's thighs. She does not object to his act of familiarity.

'What do you want to know.' It is Sonia who initiates the conversation.

'See, I have told you my impression of you, now it is your turn to tell me, so, what were your first impressions and has there been any change,' Rahul gambles with newly acquired confidence. He looks up, and it is a very romantic pose. Ranjha and Heer[127].

Rahul asks Sonia to be honest.

'You are sure, you want to know'. It is Sonia's way of getting back at him.

'Well, yes, things can't be that bad.' Rahul laughs. However, there is a perceptible drop in his confidence. What if Sonia has nothing nice to say? What if she says something he does not like?

Meanwhile, Sonia takes time to compose her thoughts. The wait makes Rahul tense. If she has to arrange her thoughts, then it can only be bad.

Sonia starts and Rahul listens.

'Well… first impressions… When I came here, and I was waiting in your house… you came and at least you were polite enough to say hello… I realised that you

---

[127] Another legendry lovers who could not unite.

were not cold or immune to my charms.' She smiles, 'I saw you hesitating and fumbling… I knew you were not your natural self. I thought you will be a lively person and a good company for my time in this city… well, I must say I have been proven right… you are not handsome or hot but let's say, ok to look at.'

Sincerely there was nothing exciting in what she was telling Rahul.

'After all this time we have been together, I think I now know and understand you a hell lot better.'

'What's your final judgment', Rahul probes further. He does not want to miss the opportunity to know what Sonia thinks of him.

'Well, you are confident, you plan your moves… you are emotional but hard-hearted at times… shrewd when you want to be… otherwise, you are a happy-go-lucky person. And with a lot of negatives attached', Sonia pauses.

'I am interested more in the negatives than the good things. People normally do not talk about the not-so-nice things, but I think you can be honest here … prove me right.' Rahul throws another challenge to her.

'You are too practical. You rarely try understanding your own emotions forget about understanding someone else's emotions.. You think you understand, but you don't. It looks like you fear that understanding other's emotions will make you weak. It will be bad for you. You will not think twice while hurting someone….

whereas you will never understand if your actions are hurting someone. Even if you know you have hurt someone, you will post rationalise.'

It was getting hard for Rahul. He did not bargain for this serious analysis. It hurt because it was so accurate.

'You think you are god's gift to girls and expect every girl to fall for your charms… and yes, your command on the language is pathetic.' Sonia stops.

'Thanks.' Rahul says softly.

'Now that I have told you all, you tell me what impressions you had of me, and I will try to see and understand you… as I know myself best.' Sonia is confident and transparent. It seems a very natural and a sincere request.

This is the last chance for Rahul to get even with her. He has the liberty to tell whatever he wants. Rahul stares at her, trying to read her face and then he starts, 'The first time I saw you sitting, you looked far more beautiful than now… I honestly thought how good it will be if I can add you to the list of the girls that I have won over… I think If you were going to be here for such a short time… I will play cool with you… maybe just flirt… maybe, get what I want.'

He paused to rearrange his thoughts and check if Sonia was offended with his statements. He sees no reaction and that could be a problem.

'Now I know you better, and I will like us to be good friends if nothing else. Let me be honest. I am infatuated with you, your beauty and the sensuous curves that leave nothing to the imagination. You have given this young lad many sleepless nights.'

Rahul sensed Sonia's momentarily stopped playing with his hair. But, she again started massaging his head. 'Till yesterday, all I wanted was to kiss you, to feel you. I had to hold myself back.' Getting confident with time, he finally asks the question in his mind. 'Tell me if last night I would have held you and kissed you… what would have been your reaction?'

'Good question', is her short reply.

'I don't think you would have raised an alarm. That would have worked against you. In this patriarchal society, people would have found faults with you. They would have said, you pushed me. the residents of this *mohalla*[128] know, how disciplined, honest and nice I am, they would agree, everyone would blame you for leading me.'

'I would have stopped meeting you.' Sonia said.

'Till yesterday, it would not have meant much to me,' he lets the statement float.

There is silence. Someone has to take charge.

'But I thought the convent girls were fast.' Rahul tries to justify his statement.

'Well, all are not made of the same wood… yes, some of the girls at the hostel are that type, and that's what

---

[128] locality

creates this stereotype impression.... they live in isolation. They are easy to be led astray... they get infatuated with false love... they can't understand the difference between love and lust... I will not be surprised if they exactly know what they are doing... and in fact, making a fool of the guys... that is their life, and I have nothing against it... however, girls who are day scholar, like me, are not that kind... we know the society... we respect the restrictions and do not fall prey to guys.'

'But what's wrong in kissing?' Rahul was not going to leave the topic so quickly... it had taken all of his confidence and courage to even speak the word.

'I want my lips, body and soul for the man who will conquer me... till now it is me who dictates... I have the upper hand with the boys... they die for one smile... what to say about kissing.'

'So, would you kiss me, or I am waitlisted.'

'No, and it is not because I cannot kiss you, but because I do not want to... you are smart enough to be my friend, and I resent that feeling of being friends only.'

'You may feel whatever you want, but I do not have such an issue. Today I will kiss you and kiss you right now.' Rahul shifts his body weight to face her, 'I consider kiss to be....'

'To be...' she repeats after him trying to gain time

'A better expression of care and love,' having said it, Rahul gets up and holds her face bringing his lips closer to her lips. Rahul feels a mild resistance from her but he refuses to stop. Soon his wet mouth meets her unresponsive lips.

Rahul stops and stares into her eyes.

He can see passion building up and feel her lips quiver. It did not matter. He kisses her again.

This time, the feeling is entirely different. Her lips are soft and full of desire, and she is kissing back. They both are hungry. Each one of them pretending as if it was not their first kiss. Trying to impress each other with their expertise. The result, their first kiss is a perfect bookish one.

After a long time, Rahul lets go of Sonia.

'Why did you not stop me?' Rahul asks.

He regrets asking the question. You don't ask such a stupid question to a girl you have just kissed

'Well, it seemed that the kiss was very important to you… it is something you were fighting for… you won me with your tenderness and brutality…' Sonia rationalises and stops short of blaming him for the episode.

'Is this to satisfy my male ego or the truth?'

'Truth.'

'Then dear, I must kiss you again,' saying this, Rahul moves forward, and she meets him halfway.

This time the kiss is entirely different. Rahul allows his hands to trespass the otherwise prohibited curves of her body. His hands slide inside her kameez and feel her tits through the fabric of her bra. He can feel her nipples, and he wants to suck on them. His amateurish untrained hands try opening the bra. Sonia stops him. She holds his hand and gets back to kissing.

***

'Sonia, I think I love you,' Rahul announces to no one in general.

'The day you are sure, tell me, in my case I know, I don't know, and I am not worried about it.'

'Then what was all this.'

'Whatever you make of it.'

***

Rahul wants time to stand still… but it is getting late.

'Don't say bye today or it will spoil the day,' Rahul requests.

He tries getting up to leave, and she holds him back.

What was that? What happened?
I know I could have held him back.
I could have stopped him and he would have stopped.
But, I am not sure if I wanted him to stop.
I wanted time to stand still and to be with him.
But, I also had to control the instinct
of flowing with the moment.
What is this? Is it love? Or is this lust?

- Sonia

Heat Flows

Rahul is in his favourite place, the dreamland. He hugs Sonia, and his intentions are no longer innocent. In his dreams, Sonia behaves differently. She encourages and aggressively desires him. Rahul softly kisses her as she guides his hands to unexplored zones, and he feels her moistness.

At the same time, he feels soft hands on his forehead. It is a very real feeling. His dream is broken as he slowly opens his eyes. Sonia is looking at him; there is love in her eyes... It is a different Sonia; this time, it is reality and no dream.

***

'You lazy bum... it is already ten, and you are still sleeping,' Sonia starts to pull the bedsheet.

'Don't,' He screams.

'Why.'

'Just leave it.' He shouts at her.

She realises the possibilities and stops pulling the bedsheet. Rahul wraps the bed sheet around and stays put.

'Get up and come... I will be at home... waiting for you.' She leaves without a backward glance. Good that Sonia left the room; otherwise, Rahul and the state of his manhood and the after-effects of the erotic dream would have embarrassed him.

After a luxurious bath, hair held in place with Brylcream and an overdose of deodorant that is also his perfume, Rahul hurries to meet her. He finds Sonia drying her hair. Her back is towards the gate. Rahul cautiously opens the gate, careful not to make any noise and slowly reaches for her. He is still staring at her creamy back when she turns around. Rahul's eyes can't hide what is in his mind. She looks enchanting, and Rahul is again fully aroused.

***

'I will be back in some time, just forgot to pick up something from home.' Rahul thinks of an excuse to get away.

'Don't I know what's troubling you?'

'No, you don't.' He is irritated

'You think a girl at sixteen will not know?'

'If you know it so well, then at sixteen, you would also know what to do about it.' Rahul teases her.

'*Dhut,* you are always in a hurry.' She seductively takes two steps, comes near him, and gently kisses him on the lips. Her hand slowly and intentionally brushes the front of his trousers. Her hand presses his manhood for that fraction of a second, and Rahul feels the heat leaving him. It is a happy ending kiss.

***

'That taken care of.' Sonia says with a twinkle in her eyes. And then she adds, 'I am sure you now want to go home and come back in some time.'

Heart Talk

The countdown for Sonia to leave town has started, and Rahul decides to spend as much time with her as possible. Both know that soon a moment will come when they will have to face unanswered questions. They must be honest with each other, even if no commitments are made. Experience is a different thing, but expectations come uninvited.

***

Rahul is at Sonia's house.

'Will you tell me something' Sonia asks.

'I will try.'

'You not sure' she teases.

'I don't know what you may be asking.'

'Oh.'

'And there might be a few things I might not be able to answer, but I will definitely try.'

'That's like a good boy,' she places his copy of poems before him.

Rahul stares at the open page. Right on the top is written, 'In Memory Of The Most Beautiful Girl I Have

Ever Met.' He was not prepared for it. In the past, whenever he visited these pages, a spectrum of conflicting emotions flooded his mind.

'What would you like to know?'

'Who was this girl?'

'She was my classmate, and I was infatuated with her… her tenderness, care and love.'

'Just infatuated? You are silly, and you are cute. You and your male ego. You can't write like this for a girl unless she means a lot to you.'

'You want cold facts,' Rahul wants to open up.

'Yes,' Sonia is confident of herself.

For Rahul, it is a challenge. He, like always, is unsure of things. Does he have the guts to share his life with her?

'Okay, She is the one responsible for what I am today. She has been a source of motivation and inspiration, and she helped me realise my potential. Currently, she is studying at Engineering College, and we are in touch.'

'Wow, she must have been an item.'

'You mean beautiful,' Rahul corrects her, not liking the word 'item.'

'Can you show me her photograph and her letters?'

Rahul takes the copy and opens the brown cover - three letters come out. He knew he could share them with her.

'And the photograph.' Sonia is not the one to give up easily.

'You can see them anytime at my place.'

'Did you lust for her.' Sonia wants to know more. Maybe the last evening incident has ignited her interest in the subject.

'If you mean lust the act... No... But if you mean as an expression of an emotion… yes.'

'I don't understand you,' Sonia is puzzled.

'Well, I was and maybe am still attracted to her… but lust is what I feel for you... and I feel more than just lust for you… And yes, I feel more drawn to you physically than to her. And forget it. It will never make sense to you.'

'I know I felt it the last time,' she smiles, 'but hell, how do you differentiate between the two.'

'Love is an emotional thing. It is like total surrender, and sex is just an act of intimacy…sexual attraction is omnipresent, and love needs the wavelength to match.'

'But unconditional surrender is not right if you ask me,' she counters his statement.

'I agree, and I never want an unconditional surrender… sacrifice without return is not my policy.' As soon as Rahul said the words, he knew his words they could initiate another tangential discussion and give rise to too many more questions.

Why can't he think before he speaks? Why does he always get into such a situation? Someday it will fuck his happiness… however, Sonia decides not to pursue the subject.

***

It is time to move on.

Rahul makes some excuses about pending work at home but promises to be back later at night. He feels their friendship has crossed the line of no return, and it is no longer just an infatuation… is this love? Possible, but he is unsure. He understands that two young teenagers can fall in love without knowing it.

***

In the evening, as luck would have it, they are alone.

Rahul remembers Sonia not resisting the kiss yesterday. In fact, she did kiss him back. Was that in some way her giving him permission to further test the boundaries?

Today, Rahul sees an invitation in her eyes, he opens his arms, and she willingly comes in. He finds her lusty lips and can feel her nipples hardening, and Rahul needs no further encouragement. Taking full advantage of the situation, his hands start moving, and soon there is nothing between his hands and her supple breast. He senses her pulling him, and everything is magically synchronised.

Confident Rahul lowers her onto the bed and looks into her eyes. It is all there; he can sense she is ready and maybe wants him to take the final steps.

Rahul finds the zip and slowly pulls open her top. His eager hands have free access to her naked tits, and he is impatient. His hand moves southwards to find the string of her Salwar, and just then, Sonia stops him.

'Not now.'

'What's wrong… this may be the only private moments we will ever manage.' He tries reasoning with her.

'No, nothing is wrong… I understand, but I feel guilty.' Tears roll down her cheeks. Rahul tenderly licks them and makes no move to leave- till she shouts, 'Leave me alone.'

She pushes him almost violently. He realises how near he was, but he also understands where she is coming from. He reluctantly leaves.

***

Rahul remembers, Sonia said - not now. It means the doors were not shut. The possibility exists. Maybe he was rushing her; perhaps he could have waited a bit more. He better find the time and a place before she changes her mind. Today she was willing, wanting and waiting, but the situation was not the best.

Who knows what tomorrow holds for them?

At home, Rahul tries to make sense of what is happening in his life. He has genuinely started liking Sonia, and he cares for her.

Nothing is in his control right now, and all he can do is wait.

Thinking of her, Rahul deep dives into sleep, and soon he is in dreamland. There, he picks up the threads. Sonia, of his dreams, is an ever-willing partner in his adventures. His fantasy has no boundaries, and soon enough, he reaches the climaxes of his senses.

No, I am not selfish.
No, I never had a second thought about
losing my virginity to Rahul.
I wanted him, but can't think of doing so.
I don't know why, but with Rahul,
I forget the space and time I am in.
I want to hold him, cuddle him and I want to take him in.
I don't think I will regret even if it is just one night stand.
I am not expecting something lifelong from him.
Maybe it will happen before I leave Agra, the city of love.
But, I know maybe it is me who will have to make the move.

- Sonia

Time Out

The first-time visitor to Agra has few destinations marked for sightseeing. Taj dominates the list, with Fatehpur Sikri, Agra Jail and Red Fort on the to-visit list. It is rare for a person not to carry back overhyped memories of the Taj and the famous Agra ka Petha[129].

Sonia is a first-time visitor to Agra and has yet to visit these places.

***

Rahul lives in Agra, yet he has been to the Taj only twice. Once when he accompanied visitors and acted as a tourist guide. And once in Grade four, when he was unaware of the monument's significance.

Maybe there is a conspiracy against the students. When they reach higher classes and start appreciating gender polarity and the concept of love and sex, schools take them to Agra jail and Fatehpur Sikri but not Taj. Rahul fails to understand the logic.

Sonia is getting anxious as the days pass. Will her visit to Agra be over without her visiting the Taj? What will

---

[129] A speciality sweet dish of Agra. Petha is a soft translucent candy from Agra. Usually rectangular or cylindrical, it is made from the ash gourd vegetable (also known as winter melon or white pumpkin),

she tell her friends that she went to Agra but did not visit Taj? And the Taj is so near that one can see the faint outlines of it from Rahul's terrace.

In the evening, while they are having tea at Sonia's place, her uncle Subhash gives Rahul the responsibility of taking the family to the Taj. Rahul, like a disciplined boy, accepts the task.

Taj Mahal, Taj as it is called, is considered a symbol of love, making it a perfect place for Rahul and Sonia to visit. However, with the previous night's events fresh in his mind, he is uneasy facing Sonia. But Sonia behaves as if nothing happened.

Rahul is back to his analyst act, with more questions than answers.

Are lust and sex the same as love? Is physical intimacy an essential requirement or just a natural expression of love? Was Sonia a wanting and a willing party to last night's incident? Is she just a tease from convent school playing with a helpless victim of her charms? What does she really want? Isn't honour not dearer than everything else? Has Rahul pushed Sonia into a corner where she had no option? What is right, and what is wrong?

Rahul knows there are no clear-cut answers. At least he does not know the answers, and there is no one he can ask.

***

The whole family starts on their historical trip to the Taj. Rahul knows the shortcuts through the lane that could have saved them some time, but he decides not to use them. However, before they can find a pedal rickshaw to take them to the Taj, they must walk to the main *chouraha*[130].

Sonia keeps pace with Rahul, and Rahul senses she is trying to gain his attention. She even tries holding his hand, and Rahul is uncomfortable with it. It is Agra, and the family is just a few steps behind them.

Rahul manages to keep a safe distance between Sonia and him. She smiles. She wants to know what his problem is? Why is he behaving the way he is? But Rahul is in his own world of emotional turbulence and refuses to acknowledge her attempts to make peace.

Sonia finally gives up and slows down. She isolates herself from the family, trying to answer her own set of questions. Her questions are not much different than Rahul's, and like Rahul, she has no one to seek answers.

Last night, what she did, was it right? Does she really love him? If this is love and an expression of affection, is love making a natural culmination of the desire?

After some time, Rahul slows down, and Sonia soon catches up with him.

'Why are you walking alone,' Rahul asks her, even when he knows the answer.

---

[130] Intersection of two roads.

'Can't I walk alone,' she reacts. There is a tinge of anger in her voice.

'When you are in a group, you must behave like a member of the group,' he advises.

'Sorry, I just don't want to… for a change. I want my privacy.'

'As you like,' Rahul drifts away and starts walking alone.

At that moment, love and Taj- seem like two extreme ends of the spectrum.

***

The group finally hired two-pedal Rickshaws. Sonia joined her mother in one, and Rahul got on the other with Ajay. Rahul is sure and uninterested in making Sonia understand his point of view. However, he is absolutely unsure if his point of view is the right point of view.

Rahul thinks that maybe Sonia regrets what transpired last evening? Or perhaps she is feeling bad because she sent him back.

Yesterday, Sonia was in his arms, and he felt her with his hands. They were so close to everything, and she most likely wanted what he desired, but the culture, society, and values may have come in the way. There cannot be any other reason for her backing out.

Rahul understood that Sonia being a girl, had much more at stake than him. Rahul is a sensible boy who will never force himself on anyone. What was happening yesterday was natural because she was willing, and it was between two consenting adults.

***

Inside the Taj complex, Rahul insists that the family hire a guide. He is not interested in doing the storytelling. If he takes on the guide role, he will be the centre of attraction, and it will be impossible for him to be alone with Sonia, even if she wishes to.

Walking down the Mughal garden, the family admires the fountains and the Nakkashi131 before climbing onto the platform. The guide gets busy explaining the making of the Taj.

You see this Taj Mahal… an excellent example of love that ever can be… not for anything but for the truth… it is one of the seven wonders of earth… It is not just an excellent architectural example… that it is… but more than that, it is an example of pure love and passion.

Rahul knows the script by heart. There is no change. The guide refers to known history and maybe what tourists want to hear. Rahul notices that Sonia, instead of giving the Taj its due attention, is watching him.

Rahul moves away, creating a clearly visible distance between them.

---

[131] The art of making flowers and creepers designed on wood or metal using a chisel and hammer.

Meanwhile, the guide continues in his typical sing-song voice.

How deep can love be... how pure it can be... a man. So, what if he was the emperor. Shah Jahan ...son of pious Mughal Emperor Jehangir... Shah Jahan made Taj in memory of his favourite queen... the ever-so-beautiful Mumtaz Mahal.

Shah Jahan met Mumtaz when he was 14 and fell in love with her. When he was 19, somewhere in 1612, he married her. She lived and loved Shah Jahan, but in 1632 after just 21 years of marriage, she died in 1631. In her memory, Shah Jahan built this wonderful Taj that you see today.

Shah Jahan, in his own words... was a good poet had said ... describing Taj

Should the guilty seek asylum here

Like one pardoned, he becomes free from sin

Should a sinner make his way to this mansion

All his past sins are to be washed away

The sight of this mansion creates sorrowing sighs

And the sun and the moon shed tears from their eyes

In this world, this edifice has been made

To display thereby the creator's glory

Why would anyone do this?

Make a monument for someone dear to you. Does one require these symbolic structures to remind them of their loved ones? If one really loved, then these monuments are of no value. One can always feel the loved one everywhere. And what is this love immortalised, Mumtaz was one of many wives of Shah Jahan, and he later married her sister. Wow, how pure was the love of Shah Jahan?

The construction of the Taj started in 1631, and it took 22000 labourers and a host of architects 22 years to complete. It is made of white marble from Makrana132 in Rajasthan and fitted with precious stones… costing 3 crore rupees then. Immediately after it was completed, Shah Jahan's son Aurangzeb put him under house arrest in Agra Fort.

*****

Sona Na Chandi Na Koi Mahal , Tujko Mai De Sakunga.

Magar Tu Carey Mujhse Mohabaat, Chota Sa Ghar Mai Dunga.

Rahul starts humming his favourite song.

Sonia, for a change, is busy listening to the guide as if someone will build a Taj Mahal for her. Rahul is silent, but the noise inside his head is tough to ignore.

Soon the visit is over, and they leave the symbol of love- the Taj behind.

*****

This trip could have been memorable for Rahul and Sonia. It is futile for Rahul to hide his feelings for Sonia. He had since long been thinking of the trip to the Taj. How will he take Sonia to the Taj and tell her what she

---

132 An area known for quality marble.

might want to hear? They will hold hands and take a picture with Taj in the background. How they will have the Banta Soda lemon or ice cream. But, on this trip, nothing like that happened. Nothing happened; the day was a complete waste. But for some different reasons and the tension they felt, it was still memorable.

Rahul leads the way back through the crowded lane away from Taj. Deep in thought, he fails to notice a pedal rickshaw coming from the other side. The Rikshawaala tries to avoid him but hits the back of Rahul's hand, and it pains.

'What happened? Does it hurt?' Sonia is immediately on his side.

'Nothing.'

'Let me see.'

'It is none of your business.'

'Does it hurt?'

'Does it matter?'

She does not like him talking to her like that.

'Let's move fast. I have to be at Anjali's place by 5 PM; she will be waiting for me.' Rahul says to irritate her.

'Oh, but Rahul, you must come back as early as possible… we have been invited for tea at your neighbours' place,' She pleads.

'So.'

'I will be waiting for you.'

'No, don't, I don't know when I will be back, and it could be very late.'

'I will wait.' Her tone has a newfound confidence, and there is something different about her.

Rahul has no answer to basic questions in his mind. What does this *Gori Ladki* want from him? What Rahul wants from her? Where will it take them? Do they have a future together?

***

If you are in a relationship, it may be an excellent time to raise and answer these questions? The questions seem simple and innocuous, but they are tough to answer.

***

Girish and Shilpa looked at each other, and Sushant could see at least there was no confusion between them.

Any other place, anyone else
and I would have given that person a real lashing.
No one dare behaves like that with me.
But, with Rahul, things are different,
don't ask me how and why.
Just understand they are different.
I know he is angry and I have a doubt that
I am the reason behind it.
It does not matter. I know, he will be back
and we will be back
picking up the threads where we left them.
But then why do I feel so helpless?
This is not love, or is it?
Or am I trying to play catch up with hostelers at my school?

- Sonia

Adventure

It took Rahul and Sonia two days to lay the foundation for it.

Rahul politely and with every bit of innocence on his face, asks his mother for advice on what he should do. He kept telling her that Sonia was making his life miserable day by day, wanting him to take her to Fatehpur Sikri. Rahul insisted that Sonia wants to see his college and visit Fatehpur Sikri; no one else in her family was interested.

Finally, Rahul's mom suggests why he does not take her to Fatehpur Sikri if no one else is interested. Rahul is happy, But once Rahul's sister knows of the plan, she too wants to go. On the other hand, the family suggests they could take the UP tourism bus starting at the Cantonment Railway station. Rahul is absolutely against it. Who wants to travel in overcrowded, rickety buses? And why is everyone concerned about how they go?

In a moment of sheer courage, Rahul declares he will take Sonia on his bike, and if anyone else wants to join them at the Fatehpur Sikri, they can take the bus. Sonia and Rahul's sister exchange glances. There is a nodding of heads. And suddenly, his sister is no longer interested in the trip. Rahul notices the change and exchange of glances between Sonia and his sister.

***

Fatehpur Sikri, the fortified city, was the short-lived capital of Emperor Akbar between 1571 and 1585. It is 44 Km East of Agra. To reach it, you must take the SH39133 and NH21134. It is almost a straight road after turning left at the Shah Ganj Police Chowki135. The road is also known as Bikaner Agra, Jaipur Agra or Fatehpur Sikri road. It is not in the best of conditions. Even in the best of times, the short ride takes more than one-and-a-half-hour, one way, without stopping.

Fatehpur Sikri town access is controlled through multiple Darwaza136. The town is so constructed that the movement gets constrained as one keeps venturing inside towards the central area reserved for the nobles. Many of these Darwaza are named by the cities they connect, like the Delhi Darwaza, Ajmer Darwaza or Gwalior Darwaza.

***

Sonia and Rahul leave Agra around 930 A.M. Sonia is wearing a pink salwar kameez with a yellow Dupatta and flat sandals. The set of Green Lakh[137] bangles

---

[133] Uttar Pradesh State Highway 39
[134] National Highway 21 Joins Bareilly in the eastern end to Jaipur on the western end.
[135] Police post.
[136] Gateways- doors.
[137] Wax- a particular type for the making of bangles- is somewhat similar to what is used to seal the envelopes.

Rahul bought from the pavement market near the Taj for her adorn on her slim Gori wrist. She sports a Rayban to protect her eyes from the scorching sun.

When they leave for Fatehpur Sikri, Sonia sits on the bike with her legs on one side. The way women typically pillion ride in India. They have mast Aloo Parantha with Curd at the famed old Madhuban Dhaba. She sits comfortably, holding on to Rahul for the onward journey with her legs on both sides of the bike.

The ride is reasonably smooth. At times, Sonia rests her cheek on his shoulder, and once or twice it seemed to Rahul that she kissed his shoulders a few times. But he could not be sure of it.

***

It takes them more than two hours to reach the tourist area at Fatehpur Sikri complex, where they realise it is closed. As far as Rahul knew, Fatehpur Sikri was one of the few tourist places open all days of the week. But, as luck would have it, today, it is closed for some work.

Rahul's first reaction is that the trip is a complete waste of time. Sonia's expression says it all; Rahul should have checked. On the other hand, pragmatic Rahul gets busy thinking of ways to make the best out of what seems a hopeless situation. He tries negotiating with the guard. He gives an emotional angle to the whole story, telling the guard they have come from a long distance. If they cannot see the inside of Fatehpur Sikri, maybe they will never get a chance to see it again.

Rahul further nudges the guard, assuring him no one would ever know. After much haggling and pleading, they strike a deal. Rahul pays the guard twenty rupees and leaves his driving license as security. The complex's main gate remains padlocked, but the guard helps them through a small opening. While they smile as they enter the complex, the guard makes it clear that if someone catches them, he will deny any arrangement.

Rahul is okay with it, and Sonia is enjoying the adventure.

The guard gives a final bit of advice, telling them to return well before the change of guards at 4 PM; otherwise, they might have to pay the other guard too.

What was a problem a few moments back is now an opportunity. Rahul and Sonia have free access to the complex, and hopefully, there will be no one to disturb them.

***

They move in from the Agra gate, and Rahul is willing to be the guide for the day. Anyway, they have no option. They cross the Kotwali[138] and, after passing the Serai[139], reach the Tansen Baradari[140]. They don't waste much time and hit for the grand view of the Sikri village and Delhi Darwaza from Day-Bungalow.

---

[138] Police station.

[139] A place to stay – for the travellers.

[140] Tansen was one of the nine gems of Akbar's court and was the court musician and singer. Fatehpur Sikri – Tansen's Baradari is his residence, but it is disputed. It is small in size for a nobleman of his stature. It seems it gets its name because it has twelve doors.

Soon they are at Hauz-i-Shirin, the tank with sweet water and are surprised to find water in the tank, though they are unwilling to taste it. After moving from one part of the complex to the other, they decide to rest. They find the steps under the welcome shadow of the large Jamun tree and sit down, holding hands. They are finally at ease with each other.

***

Rahul, the guide, tells Sonia the story of Fatehpur Sikri.

Once, Badshah Akbar visited Sikri village, where the renowned Sufi saint Shaikh Salim Chishti foretold him of the birth of his son and heir to the Mughal throne. Akbar was thrilled when the prophecy came true. After Jahangir's second birthday, Akbar started the construction of his second capital at Fatehpur Sikri.

***

All areas inside the complex are closed, including the museum, which is anyway not of much interest to them. They peep into the Daulat Khanna[141] and Haran Sara, the oldies' quarters.

Sonia playfully does a delicate Adaab[142] to Badshah Rahul as they stand on the vast platform near the centre of the complex. She smiles and winks at the Badshah, who likes what the begum is doing. He holds her at the wrist to pull her in.

---

[141] Daulat Khana (Imperial Palace) comprises three distinct sections: the Royal Library (Kutub-Khanah), Akbar's Atelier (Citra Sala) and the imperial apartments (Khwabgah) constructed in 1572.
[142] The Muslim way of greeting.

***

They are on the slightly raised platform at the Imperial Place complex; Begam Sonia is in the arms of Badshah Rahul. It is like Mughle-Azam[143]; her face tilted like Madhubala[144]. Her eyes closed in expectations, completely surrendering to her lover Prince Salim.

The lover leans in to meet Begam's lips. The kiss feels different; it is not stolen or requested and happens naturally.

They complete their tour of the complex after seeing the two most famous structures at Fatehpur Sikri. The Buland Darwaza and the Tomb of Shaikh Salim Chishti. The Buland Darwaza is an enormous and impressive site, but the Tomb is closed for renovation. They miss the chance to seek the saints blessing for their undeclared love.

Their mood is excellent, and the weather plays the perfect host.

Finally, they walk past the local market parallel to the fort's walls. As the complex is closed for renovation, there are very few shops that are open selling mementos that tourists would typically buy. Rahul ends up buying a blue coloured stone necklace and places it around Sonia's neck. The central pendant,

---

[143] One of the iconic films of Indian Cinema, based on the love story of Salim (Akbar's son) and a dancer in the royal court.
[144] The famous and one of the most beautiful actresses ever in Indian Cinema. She played the role of Anarkali in the movie.

shaped like a heart, precariously hangs near her cleavage, threatening to drop in.

They finally end their trip with snacks at the Jodhabai[145] Restaurant. Topping it with ThumsUp. And they are finally all set to return. They would have wanted more time between them, but then there was the long ride home.

***

On the way back, Sonia sits with her legs on both sides of the bike, tightly holding on to Rahul and naturally leaning on to him. Her hands wrapped around his waist. This time, Rahul had no doubt that Sonia's wet lips kissed his back.

On the way back, just before the Airport colony, Sonia asks Rahul to stop. She changes her position and is back to pillion riding with her legs on one side of the bike. They will soon be entering the city.

Rahul understands. She was pressing onto him because she knew no one would notice. In the city, she has to sit in a *sanskari*[146] way. Sonia, however, holds on to Rahul, and he needs no further proof of Sonia's feelings. He is sure he is not a time-pass for the convent-educated Sonia.

---

[145] Jodhabai was the Rajput Princess Badshah Akbar married- she was also the mother of Prince Salim.
[146] The cultured and socially appreciated way.

The trip to Fatehpur Sikri was so nice.
Rahul and me alone on the bike.
He riding it hard like every male of his age would do with a
girl pillion riding.
The time at the Sikri, so nice.
God, why did we take so much time to express ourselves?
Wait, do I really think I love him?
Am I sure we have expressed our feelings?

- Sonia

Apology

The day is almost over, and the Sun starts to set behind Taj. Today Rahul and Sonia have not met. Sonia had not attempted to contact Rahul, even when she knew he was at home and waiting for her. In the battle of egos, both of them were losers. None of them wanted to be the first to offer a truce.

***

Rahul is doomed. His exams can be announced any day, and if he does not focus on his studies, his rank might slip. Fun is great, and love – romance are important, but studies and a bright future are always priorities.

He takes out his long-neglected books and tries to study. However, his restless mind keeps wandering to the day before. Sonia dominates his thoughts, and he is unable to concentrate. So, he does the second-best thing. He starts making notes. In reality, copying the text from the books onto his notebook. It helps, but the magic does not last long. Sonia once again enters his thoughts uninvited. He starts thinking about what Sonia could be thinking and what could have stopped Sonia from contacting him.

Sonia, meanwhile, is waiting for him. Against her nature, she had tried her best to make stubborn Rahul talk in an attempt to mend the broken fence of their blossoming relationship.

How far will she go if Rahul refuses to reciprocate?

Her thoughts and emotions are in conflict with her heart.

Is Rahul only interested in her body? She discards the thought. Her Rahul is not like others. And she is absolutely sure about it. A girl has many ways to know when a boy is interested in her and what interests him.

Sonia decides to give it one final try. If not Rahul and his love, she still wants to take sweet memories from Agra. Soon, she will leave, and maybe they will never meet. Sonia picks the copy of the poems and starts for Rahul's home. Anyway, she has to return the goddamn notebook.

***

The main door is open. Sonia presses the bell but does not wait for any response. She knows Rahul is at home, and aunty (Rahul's mother) is most likely on her evening walk. In the last few weeks, Sonia has almost become a part of the family, and she knows every family member's schedule.

She walks in and, for a change, finds Rahul is studying. She hesitates and then, in mock anger, slaps the book on his thighs. After having done her bit, she turns to leave.

A small piece of paper drops from the book, it reads 'you are so rude- Sorry.'

Oh Shit. What is this?

Rahul follows Sonia, and by the time he reaches the main door- Sonia is on the road, walking away.

***

Rahul quickly evaluates his options. He can follow her; maybe it will make her feel better. She has already done what she could, and his anger may not be justified. Rahul smiles; everything is not yet lost, and there is nothing mine or yours in love.

He finds her at her home. She is smiling. Is that the smile of victory, sarcasm or invitation?

'What do you mean by this' Rahul pushes paper under her eyes.

'What does it say.'

'So, I am rude.'

'Yes.'

'But why sorry.'

'Because you are angry with me.

'Oh, forget it,' Rahul finds it unimportant.

'I understand, Rahul. Everyone needs private moments. But one needs to come out of their shell and not allow the moments to be wasted… think about it, Mr Rahul,' saying this, she takes the piece of paper, crumples it and throws it towards the waste paper basket. The paper does not go in, Rahul, the cricketer, picks it up and drops it into the basket.

Rahul tries to justify his behaviour, 'I do need some private moments, and so I must be leaving.'

'You are making me again feel guilty.' Sonia accuses Rahul of hurting her. Her eyes have that look. It is a tough call for Rahul to stay or to leave.

'No, not-at-all… it's the reality, and yes, I do have some jobs to do.'

'Sure,' she seeks confirmation, but her eyes ask, if so, why the hell has he followed her.

'Sure,' he kisses her on the forehead and leaves.

***

Rahul knew Sonia wanted him to stay back. He also knew that Sonia was confident; he would stay if she asked. But, sometimes, you have to lose a bit to win in the end. He knew, finally, the dice had rolled in his favour.

Passion

On Monday, Rahul's and Sonia's Mother are off to Shiva Mandir. Her brother Ajay is with his friends in the neighbourhood, and Rahul's sister is in school. Sonia is at Rahul's place. She has offered to keep the breakfast ready by the time the senior ladies return from the temple.

Sonia is busy in the kitchen, and Rahul is busy reading the newspaper.

After some time, Sonia brings him *aloo sabzi*[147] and *poori*[148]. She stands there waiting for his reaction.

'How is it?' she asks.

'Good… tasty.'

'Good.'

'No excellent.'

'That's like a good boy. Fast learner.'

'What do you mean' Rahul counters her statement.

'Do you think your mom will like it?'

---

[147] A dry dish made with potato
[148] Deep-fried flat rounds of wheat flour bread.

'Sure, she will. But why is it important for you whether she likes it or not? She is not seeing a girl for me.'

'Well, there is nothing wrong in having a good first impression? … it may help in future.'

'Oh, like that.'

'Yes, like that.' She winks and plants a hurried kiss on his forehead.

Rahul knows it is Sonia's way of acknowledging her feelings. He holds her hand and kisses her fingers. He looks up and finds her lips waiting for him. Finally, they kiss. Rahul holds Sonia by her waist and pulls her toward himself. Things take time to warm up, and soon they lose their sense of timing and space.

'Now.' She says.

'What.' Rahul fails to understand her hint.

'Rahul… now… take me, Rahul… make me yours.'

It takes Rahul a few moments to understand. He fumbles with her dress, but she patiently guides him. He tries opening her bra but fails; she laughs, slips her arms and pulls the bra so that the hooks are now in the front, and then she waits for Rahul to do the honours. She helps Rahul out of his T-shirt, the trousers are gone in a jiffy, and Rahul focuses on opening her salwar.

'Rahul, close the door.'

'Oh … leave it… who is coming.'

'If someone does.'

'Well, if it's an outsider, I expect to hear the bell,' Rahul whispers while kissing her. 'and if it is my or your mom… well, they will not ring the bell for sure… but a closed-door will tell them the story anyway.'

'Shut up.'

'Yes, Sonia… I am concentrating.' His hands find her moist patch.

They soon get busy exploring each other. It takes Sonia time to find enough confidence to reach down and hold him. She is anxious and fears the pain but knows she must guide Rahul in.

She bites her lips as he enters her, and Sonia is no longer a virgin. Rahul realises he is the first man for her, and Sonia instinctively knows she is the first for him.

Between the two inexperienced lovers, there is nothing more to say.

Their bodies soon find a natural rhythm seeking unknown pleasure. Rahul climaxes as Sonia holds him tight while he tries a few more feeble pushes. Their hard breathing punctuates the blissful pin-drop silence in the room.

***

Sonia snuggles close to Rahul and holds him tight. They have been lucky to be alone and luckier that no one turned up while they were busy in the act. They realise they must dress up. Together they check the room and remake the bed erasing any tell-tale signs of their passionate act.

By 1030 A.M, the ladies are back. Rahul can feel his mother scrutinising him. Satisfied, she relaxes. Rahul and Sonia look at each other and share a smile; their act is a secret between them, and the elderly ladies have no clue what happened sometime back.

***

Sonia, like a nice, disciplined daughter, serves breakfast. Rahul does not join as his hunger is taken care of. He tells his mother, 'I had my breakfast… she is good… I loved it.' He smiles at Sonia. Fortunately, no one catches Sonia blushing. She leaves the room to get some more sabzi. And while she crosses Rahul, she bites her tongue and winks at him.

***

It finally happened.
I am no longer a virgin and I have given myself to Rahul.
Time will tell if that has been a right or a wrong decision.
We are too young and there are many years for togetherness.
Many if's, but, parantu[149] and lekin[150]
between the possibilities.
But, living in the present, I am happy.

- Sonia

---

[149] Replacement or equivalent of But, still, yet, nevertheless or however-more as an explanation of a reason, excuse, or doubt
[150] Another Hindi expression of doubt- equivalent of But, still, yet, nevertheless or however- more as an explanation of a reason, excuse, or doubt

Precaution

The family stays over for lunch. Rahul and Sonia find time to be together- however, Rahul could feel that Sonia is not her usual self. She is tense, and has been trying to find some private moment with Rahul, who signals her to wait.

It is post-lunch when they find a moment alone.

Sonia nervously tells Rahul. 'Oops, we forgot protection- what if I get pregnant?'

Yes, we did, but how was I to know that we would end up making love.'

'You should have thought of it.'

'You should have told me, warned me that you were planning to seduce me,'

'I seduced you.' There is a surprise in her voice, but she knows better.

'Yes, you did.'

'No, you started.'

'You could have stopped me.'

There is silence between us.

'Forget that- the important thing is, What if I get pregnant.'

'No, I withdrew in time.'

'Don't lie; you did not.'

'You are unnecessarily getting tense and spoiling the blissful feeling.'

'You don't understand.'

'Don't worry. If you do get pregnant, we will see.'

'What! - don't even say that.'

'If you miss your periods, then we will know.'

'Oh, my periods are due in a few days.'

'Let us wait.'

'No, don't worry; I wanted to see your reaction. I know I am nearing my date, so the chance of pregnancy is low.'

'Oh.'

'Yes, being a girl, we know these things.'

'I am enlightened.' Rahul smiles.

'But, if I miss my periods, you will be the one who will have to get me the pill.'

'Done. I love you.'

'I love you too.'

***

Finally, they said the magic words both wanted to hear. It happened at the spur of the moment, and there it was, pure 24-carat. They were in love, and it needed no explanation.

Rahul held her hand, and she leaned on to him.

***

'When I will leave, will you forget me?' Sonia whispers.

'Stupid, why do you say so? We will remain in touch.'

'How.' She wants details.

'Through letters.'

'As if your mother will allow it', her doubts surface.

'Why, she does not need to know.'

'In that case, I will write to you, and you write to me.'

'That is what I am saying.' Rahul is calm and composed.

'Okay, done. I will give you the address tomorrow.'

***

Time Over

Sonia is leaving Agra today, and Rahul's family is at Subhash's place to send them off. Rahul intentionally stays back at his home. He is having a conversation with himself. He is more rational than emotional for his age, but then he is human, and love is a funny emotion.

There is something between them- no point giving it a name. Maybe it is love... and if it is love, sooner or later, it will win... win what... nothing... he knows nothing. It will overcome distances and separation. They are too young for a long-term distant relationship and commitment, but the intent is right.

Love happens like that. Let's see what happens in the future. After all, it is time that has all the answers. Life with Sonia was no different; life without Sonia will not be different.

***

Sonia serves tea to Rahul's mother and sister, who have come to say goodbye. She knew Rahul would not come, he had told her yesterday, but her eyes kept searching for him. Sonia had laughed and told him not to be kiddish, not to be an emotional fool.

She surprised Rahul by telling him, 'Don't worry if this love fails or if you don't love me, I love you, and that is important to me. And If I still get pregnant and you are not there to help me, I will manage.'

'You are my first love.' Rahul says to her.

'Thanks. You could have said, I am your first mistake. But I want to be your last love.'

'oh!.'

The conversation last night left too many maybe's open in the discussion. Something both of them were avoiding addressing. Anyway, it was not the time to address such questions.

***

Sonia knew there was no point in thinking and wasting time. She has to meet Rahul before leaving. She knew Rahul would be waiting and most likely expecting her. Rahul has not come. Most likely, he wants a few more moments in complete privacy. Alone at home now has an entirely different meaning for them.

She had questions in her mind. Can she trust Rahul? More importantly, does she trust herself? But what was there to trust? The promises have been made, and it is up to them to deliver. Both of them have been extra generous in stating that they were unsure how far the relationship would go and were not seeking any commitment.

She leaves silently without letting anyone know. Rahul is on the terrace and watches her sprint between the two houses. He hurries down the stairs and meets hers halfway through in his living room.

***

They hold each other, and she rests her head on his shoulder. He pats her head. This is the moment that will forever be embedded in their memory. Something they will cherish all their life. She plants hurried kisses on his cheeks and pulls him into her. Rahul tries reading her eyes.

'Not Now.' Sonia says, and this time Rahul understands.

'Why.' he asks, not because he wants to make love but to be absolutely sure.

'Because of my periods.'

'Oh,' was all he could say.

'Hey, that's good.'

'What's so good about it… we could have.'

'Hold, Rahul… it means I will not get pregnant.'

'Oh,' Rahul does not know how to react.

***

It is time to leave. Rahul finally agrees to come to the railway station.

When they reach the station, the train is already on the platform. After adjusting their luggage and rechecking their seats, Rahul does not wait for the train to leave. He is not comfortable seeing tears in Sonia's eyes. Maybe because Rahul is emotionally drained and worried that he may tear up. Whatever it may be, he was getting emotional and did not want Sonia to catch him weeping.

Despite what happened in the last few days, Rahul is still unsure if Sonia feels the same way about their experience. He hopes she does because he indeed loves her.

He turns towards the coffee house, knowing some of his friends will be there. An era of happiness is over, and Rahul today is lonely among his friends.

6 YEARS LATER

PART -III

THE HUNT

Afterwards

The story of Rahul and Sonia is no different than other love stories of young lovers. The pattern is the same. A promise to remain in touch is made, and they follow it up with the complete dedication and passion that a distant relationship needs. Initially, the letters are long, painstakingly crafted on special papers placed in specially bought envelopes and posted with a lingering kiss before the wait starts for the reply.

In the mid-eighties, letters were the only way to remain in touch other than the infrequent telephone calls made from the STD[151] PCO[152] booths on special occasions like birthdays. But, these calls could not be made often as everyone did not have phone connections.

There were times when the gaps between letters and calls were long. The young lovers held on to their expectations and beliefs. The letter allowed them to craftily camouflage their real feelings, as one could not write openly. However, the other lovers understood the unsaid between the lines.

---

[151] Subscriber's Trunk Dialling- STD- these were booths where people came to make calls, as people did not have landline telephone connections.
[152] Public call office.

Like everyone else, Rahul and Sonia were the victims of deep thinking. The thinking that goes, I think she thinks, that I think, she will be thinking that I will be thinking she loves me. Making assumptions in the absence of a ready means of communication. At times, the words and situations, in the absence of other things, failed to communicate emotions and were bound to be misinterpreted.

And thus, at times, the trapped emotions failed to find the valley that could amplify the echoes of their love.

Rahul and Sonia shared no picture. However, they did manage to meet a few times.

Sonia visited Agra on a short trip when Subhash got married. It was fun as the marriage provided perfect cover to the young lovers to steal many moments of hungry togetherness. They were less worried and better educated about protection. Rahul met her at Naukuchital[153] while she was on a school trip. And they did manage a few calls at her friend's home. These were lightning calls[154] and cost a bomb.

***

Slowly, Rahul and Sonia both got busy in their life. First, the number of pages in the letters dropped, then the frequency of letters decreased, and finally, one day, the letters stopped. It was complete silence. Surprisingly, neither Rahul nor Neeli felt a vacuum or the need to restart their communication links.

---

[153] One of the lakes in District Nainital, Uttarakhand.
[154] Lightening calls were urgent calls that the operator patched up on priority. It cost almost thrice the regular trunk call.

By the time Rahul finished engineering, it was already one year of no letters. He wrote one last letter to Sonia, telling her he completed Engineering with Honours. Additionally, Rahul shared with her the good news that once he is employed, they can seek their parents' blessings and start a new life together. To ensure the letter was delivered to the addressee, sent it through a registered post[155]. To his surprise, the letter returned with a remark - addressee not found.

By that time, Subhash had left Agra. However, much as Rahul tried, he failed to trace Sonia. He tried calling her home, and the person on the other side told him no one named Sonia lived there. He tried the girl's hostel, but even they had no clue. The friend's number was disconnected, and after many such efforts, Rahul gave up.

***

Post engineering, Rahul was placed with a car company in Delhi. One day, while returning from a dealer's visit at the Lajpat Nagar market, he saw Sonia entering the Women Polytechnic hostel at South Extension. There was no doubt it was Sonia. What he was unsure of was if he was still in love with her or if she still loved him.

However, seeing Sonia, his buried memories were revived, and emotions found new expressions. There

---

[155] A postal system, where you get the receipt of delivery or the department brings your letter back. It explains why it could not be delivered.

still were possibilities of togetherness, he was still single, and it was enough for him to start the chase. He wanted to meet Sonia and find out what had happened. It would help him close the chapter, or maybe it would be the start of a beautiful new chapter in his life.

He was in a hurry to meet her but not impatient. He asked his colleagues if they had friends or connections in the polytechnic hostel. He even made friends with the guard at the hostel and smoked beedi. Unfortunately, the guard did not know Sonia. There were too many girls in the hostel, and the guard only knew troublemakers or the girls who habitually came in late or who he supplied liquor. Rahul was happy that Sonia did not feature in that list.

However, his spending time with the guard was not completely wasted. The guard gave him a decent tip. Every Friday, the girls had their outing, and most would go shopping at Palika Bazaar at Connaught Place. It was crucial enough information for Rahul to gift Hariram an extra bundle of Pataka bidi.

For the next three Fridays, Rahul would take leave and park himself outside the hostel. He diligently watched the gate from 3 in the afternoon to 630 in the evening. After that, he would leave for Palika Bazaar, where he would keep moving around till the shops started closing. His hope of finding Sonia dropped with every passing week. It even made Rahul doubt if he had seen Sonia or if she was someone else. Nothing seemed to be working for him.

The story could have been different if Rahul had given up his quest. But he decided to try one last time, and this time he was lucky. He saw Sonia coming out with her friends; sure enough, they took an auto. Rahul followed.

Sonia was with her friends. She looked beautiful, and Rahul was again in love with her. True to the guard tip, the ladies got down at Janpath for their shopping. Sonia stopped to buy at a stall while her friends kept walking. She was now alone, and Rahul saw it as the right opportunity to approach her.

Before Rahul could say anything, Sonia turned and accosted him. 'So… finally, you found time to trace me.' She continued, 'Many days, I saw you standing outside the hostel. It was no brainer to realise that you wanted to meet. Today I have come only for you; my friends have carried on creating a cover for me.

'What are you saying… Sonia… I always remember you.'

'Do you… cross your heart and answer me.'

"Yes, I do,' and Rahul crossed his heart.

'But it's too late.'

'Why did you not answer my letters.'

'Because I never got them once the family moved out to Kashipur, where Dad was posted.'

'Why did you not tell me?'

'Why. Well, I did, and I wrote you letter after letter… every week… even when there was no reply from you.

'I never got any.'

'I know.'

'What do you mean? You said you wrote me letters,' things were unfolding too fast for Rahul.

'I said I knew you never got my letters, even though I had the correct address.'

"Yes, we still stay in the same house… So, what happened?'

'Do you remember your parents coming to Kashipur for one of your cousin's marriage,' Sonia asked.

'Yes.'

In addition to attending the cousin's marriage, they had another important agenda. They came to our house. Don't tell me you never knew because I know, you never knew. They had all my letters. Most of them are still unopened. Your parents read a few of them and then even stopped opening them. They were only interested in ensuring my letters did not reach you. They were successful. When they opened the bag full of my letters, full of my feelings and emotions, pain, and happiness, I realised they had something else in mind. Those were my letters to you; they were meant to be read by you.'

'Oh,' Rahul could visualise the scene at her home.

'They told my parents that they have no intention of getting us married. There is no question of waiting, no need to talk. That our love is juvenile, and they had other plans for you.

I sat there looking at my parents and pleading with your mother, but she refused to hear. She asked my parents to make sure I stopped writing letters. But your parents were not finished; they even threatened that if I continue to write or try in any way to contact you, they will ensure that the letters reach the right hands, and then no one will marry me. They ended up reiterating their point and warning me.'

'I protested.' I told them my Rahul would marry me. They laughed; that laughter still echoes in my head. They said, you will do what your mother wants, and she did not see me as a daughter-in-law. They mocked and asked me whether my Rahul had done anything when the letters stopped. And trust me, I had no answer to their questions.'

'I begged them not to be so cruel… for I love you… if, in those years, you would have done what you did today… maybe things would have been different. Maybe… but you did not… threatened by your parents, and seeing the helplessness of my parents … I had no alternative but to promise I will never write to you.'

'Oh God, all this time, I kept thinking you have changed your mind about me.'

'You are partially correct... I do love you, and I will love you till I die... this is something no one can take away from me... but I will never again meet you.'

Rahul understood. He could not find fault with Neeli's decision.

He has been the perfect mama's boy. Within himself, he knew his mother was right and that he would never go against her decision.

'Before you go... I want you to meet someone.' Sonia led him towards the coffee shop... a young man came forward. He hugged her... his protective arms around her completed the picture.

'Meet Captain Sanjay,' she paused and looked at him, 'my fiancée, and Sanjay, meet Rahul... a very dear friend... someone you know I loved.'

'Hi.' Rahul extended his hand, which was gripped hard by the Captain.

'Don't worry, Rahul... it is OK... he knows most things about you and me... I must have bored him with your stories... I wanted to start the new chapter in my life with a clean slate... and it was essential for me to share my first love with him... I did... he accepts it and considers me lucky to have met you, and I am honoured to find a person like Sanjay.'

'Yeah,' Rahul had no words.

'I think, now you can leave, but before you do... I have something that I should return to you... here is the only picture of you and me together on your terrace and a faint outline of the Taj at a distance …it was an early morning foggy day… I hope it is clear now.'

'And' Sonia continued, 'I will invite you to our marriage… more for your parents than for you… but I am sure… it is one thing they will surely share with you… but do me a favour… do not come… It has taken me ages to come out of it… I am not that strong… I would prefer if we do not test each other.'

Rahul shook hands with Captain Sanjay and looked at Sonia.

'One more promise you have to make,' she said

'Ask me… Sonia… anything.'

'Never let your parents know you know about the undelivered letters. As far as they are concerned, they were doing what they felt was right. My parents did what they believed was right. Maybe we are destined to only have those moments of togetherness. Be my Shiva. just be my Shiva[156].'

***

For the first time, Rahul understood what Sonia wanted. He promised, and as he left the lovely couple still waiting for their coffee, he remembered the days she was with him at Agra.

---

[156] Shiva is one of the three Supreme Gods of Hindu Hindi, and the other two are Vishnu and Brahma. Shiva is known to have taken the poison that came out of Samudra Manthan (the churning of the sea) and held it in his neck to protect the universe from dying.

While Rahul was narrating the last part of the story,
Sushant left the family alone.
It was their moment of realisation and a right to privacy.

BACK TO PRESENT

BACK TO PRESENT
PART- IV
PICTURE ABHI BAKI HAI

Ultimate Discovery

'So, what is all this story about.' Shilpa could not stop asking.

'You still haven't understood; I am surprised… Come on, Girish and Shilpa… do you still want a clue.' Rahul said.

'Ok, give me a clue.' Shilpa is unsure if she is the only one who does not get the story. She did not want to wait.

'What's your father's name?' Rahul questioned

'Brigadier Sanjay Jugran.'

'Oh shit… it can't be true. Is that what you telling us.' It was Girish's turn to be surprised.

'Yes, fortunately, that is the truth.' Rahul almost whispers, holding the picture.

'What is it, Girish.' Shilpa is still clueless or unwilling to accept what is clear to the rest of them.

'Shilpa, your dad, is the young Captain Sanjay, your father-in-law met at Janpath. And if you look closely…and see the picture again… you will see a face just like yours.' Rahul is going slow with the information download on a sensitive subject.

'Maa…'

'Yes, Shilpa, your mother is my first love... and just like Captain Sanjay Jugran… even I told Girish's mother about Sonia…. Somewhere we decided to see if the next generation unites the families. What if our children end up falling in love with each other? Coincidently and with some deft manoeuvring, family outings, same college etc., we managed for you both to not only meet but fall in love.'

'Oh shit.' Girish mummers. 'So ours was really an arranged love marriage.'

***

Rahul takes the picture out and flips it over. The ink is dry, and the paper is old, but the emotions are as raw as some 35 years ago.

THE GIRL

I saw her first in lovely pink,

Her fragrance put flowers to shame.

My feelings towards her are no longer the same.

She dresses like she is wearing the dew.

Inciting dreams that are not rare or few.

Love comes without calling, gives without asking.

She silently speaks with her expressive eyes.

Gracefully walks, and her talks are intoxicatingly high.

What draws us closer remains unexplained.

There is unsaid hunger in her eyes and heart.

It says the day love wins, we will be one.

And there is a secret, I must wait for the day to come.

***

Climax

Just as if on cue, the doorbell rings. It is timed to perfection.

When Shilpa opens the door, she sees a lady in a bridal dress, her face hidden behind intricate Lucknow gold zari. Sushant Chachu holding her hand, leads her in.

Shilpa is foxed. Is Sushant *Chachu* finally marrying Shormilla Aunty?

Shilpa follows the lady and keeps searching Sushant Chachu's face for an answer. As she closes the door, Sushant asks her to hold on and let Pandit Ram Milam Mishra and his assistant in the hall. Panditjee's assistant is carrying a *chowki* and *Chatai*[157].

Girish and Shilpa are clueless as to what is happening. Sushant has a naughty smile, and this time, Rahul is missing from the room.

Pandijee's assistant starts setting up for the *Havan*[158] in the garden area.

---

[157] A thin mattress made of grass.
[158] The holy fire.

Rahul steps out of his room. He is wearing a Groom's attire. Rahul is wearing a blueish Lucknawi Ackhkan and a sherawali *pagdi*[159]. He carries a *Varmala*[160] in hand.

'Papa, what is all this.' A confused Girish asks.

'What you wanted this morning.'

'What.'

'You said if I have someone in mind, I should get married.'

'Yes.'

'So, I am getting married. Do you have any objection?'

'No, but you could have told us.'

'And do what, discuss and debate. So, I did nothing.' Rahul turns to Shilpa and seeks her vote. 'Do you have any objection, Shilpa?'

'Well, fine, I don't have a Mother-in-law, now I will have one.'

'Sure.'

'Yes.'

'Without even knowing who the bride is.'

There is silence for a few moments. The whole thing could go topsy-turvy in no time.

Rahul asks Shilpa to see the bride's face and tell if his choice is good. He still has the picture in his hand.

---

[159] Ceremonial headgear.
[160] The floral necklace that the bride and the groom exchange.

The penny finally drops.

Shilpa realises what is happening and why Rahul wants her to see the face of the bride. She gasps for breath, and her expression begs someone to tell her it is not what she is thinking.

She hesitantly approaches the bride, who is comfortably sitting on the sofa. As she comes near, Sonia sees the hand and the rings on it. She needs no more clues.

Her voice trembles. 'Ma' is all she can say.

The lady opens her arms, and Shilpa sways into them.

'Maa, you are marrying Pa.'

'Yes, that's what it looks like. Tell me your father-in-law is a good choice.'

Yes, he is.'

'I know.'

'When did you decide? When did it re-start.'

'Ask your Pa.'

***

Rahul shares the secret. 'We have been together for some 2 years now. Two people with a vacuum in their lives. No, we are not disrespecting the memories of our spouses.'

'I think we came near each other after your father was martyred fighting terrorists. It was also when I was alone; we supported each other as we are *Samdhis*[161].'

'It did not take us much time to realise that we still love and need each other. The time we spent together was pure happiness. We went for a few short vacations together to check if the passion was still alive. And in a way, we rejuvenated the spirits of young Rahul and Neeli of many years back.'

Rahul had the full attention of Shilpa and Girish.

They are happy but surprised. Sushant is watching them, and Panditjee is lost. This is not what he expected when Sushant asked him to come to the Defence colony house.

'Life could have continued without any problem. But we knew that if anyone came to know about us or our plan, there would be questions and comments. And we were in no mood to accept or answer. So, we decided it is better to first get legally married and then answer the questions.'

"But why hide it? Why not do it all in the open? Why not share it with us?' It is Girish's turn to sound angry and disappointed. 'Were you not sure of our response?'

'Stop talking to your father like that.' Sonia steps into the argument. 'We knew you would not object to our marriage. However, the people marrying are your father and your wife's mother. A bit odd. So, we

---

[161] A term that means the parents from the Groom and the Bride side.

decided to give you the shortest possible reaction time.' She continues, 'That was our decision, and now you have all time to react. But nothing is going to change our decision.'

'What if I don't agree.' Girish is testing the waters.

'Nothing will happen, they will still get married…, *marriage toh ho Kar rahegi*[162]… Panditjee ready.' Sushant informs Girish and checks with Pandiji.

'I like the spirit, papa.' Girish hugs Rahul.

Shilpa takes her mother's hand, and Girish Leads Rahul towards the *Vedi*[163] and waits for Panditjee.

And who will do the Kanyadaan, Panditjee wants to know.

'I will do the *kanyadaan*[164].' Sushant steps forward, holding Sonia's hand.

***

Sonia sits on Rahul's right-hand side. Sushant ties Rahul's stole to her dupatta. They hold hands as Panditjee starts reciting mantras.

***

Rahul and Neeli finish their seven *Pheras*[165] and return to the hall with neatly packed suitcases. Before the

---

[162] Nobody can stop this marriage.

[163] In Hindu marriage, the holy fire (*Havan*) area is lit, and the Bride and the Groom take seven rounds, signifying the vows. *Vedi* is the place where the fire is lit.

[164] The person who will give away the bride in marriage.

[165] The seven circles, the Groom and the bide, walk around the sacred fire.

children could react, they tell them the recently married couple is taking the night flight to the Maldives.

Sushant winks at Rahul. *'Yaha Meri Paheli Shaadi Nahi Hui, Aur Tu.'*[166] Rahul understands and teases him, 'Sonia is my first Love-second time.'

Sonia playfully glares at Rahul. And they step out to the waiting taxi.

***

---

[166] I am yet to get married for the first time, and here you are.

I know, Shilpa will take time to react.
Her mother is now also her Mother -in-law.
Her father-in-law is her father too.
And her husband for all you can say is step brother and no
blood relation.
And my sandhi is my husband- and my Son-in-law my son.
I have no regrets and no complaints.
Whatever is to happen, happens for the better.
Even first love- second time.

- Sonia

The Secret

Sonia and Rahul had long discussions whether the children must know the complete story. The truth could really upset them. And so they decided to tell a Yudhister truth[167]. Truth but not the absolute truth.

Here is what Rahul and Neeli did not share with them.

***

After marriage, Sonia failed to conceive for a long time. Sanjay and Sonia consulted many doctors and were finally told the problem was with Sanjay. His sperm count was too low, and the army man Sanjay never took it lightly. They did discuss adoption, which Sanjay never wanted, and Sonia was against artificial fertilisation with some donor sperm. So, they decided to leave it to God and keep trying.

---

[167] King Yudhister the eldest of the Pandav's was known to only speak truth. Their guru Dronacharya was a mighty fighter- who was fighting from Kaurav's side and it was difficult to defeat him. His son was Ashwatthama and there was also a elephant with the same name. Bhima the brother of Yudhister killed Ashwatthama the elephant and shouted that Ashwatthama was dead. Dronacharya did not believe anyone and came to ask Yudhister if it was true. Yudhister is supposed to have shouted back – Yes Ashwatthama is dead and then utter under breath that he did not know if that was a an r the elephant.

At this point, Sonia realised that this lack of a child was adversely affecting her married life. Sanjay had taken it as a question mark on his manhood. And the only person who could help her with what she had in mind was Rahul.

After considering all the options with confidence and courage, she reached out to Rahul.

Sonia first called Rahul and told him she wanted a meeting. Rahul willingly agreed to come over to her city without even asking for the reason for this sudden call. There Sonia told him what she wanted him to do.

She asked for *Niyog*[168] without Sanjay's knowledge. She explained her reasons for the bold decision, and it took time for Rahul to come to terms with it. To say Rahul was shocked will be understanding. But Sonia prevailed, and Rahul agreed.

In the next few months, according to Sonia's possible ovulation dates, Rahul and Sonia made trips to Jaipur with the sole aim of getting Sonia pregnant.

***

Rahul remembered the first trip he had made with Sonia. They checked into Clarks Awad in adjacent rooms with a connecting door, and both nervously waited for the other to take the first step.

---

[168] The wilful intercourse with a close relative (not her husband) or an identified qualified person to get pregnant. It was followed earlier and was primarily done to find the inheritor to continue the lineage, with the permission of family members.

Finally, Sonia knocked at the connecting door and came over. Rahul already had a glass of whisky to help him overcome anxiety. However, Sonia was absolutely clear, what they planned must not happen under the influence of liquor. It was an open-eyed conscious decision two adults had taken, which is how it must remain.

They had been in love before. Still, in moments of weakness, they craved each other's company but never allowed it to be known. It still took time for them to get comfortable with each other before they made love.

Understandably, they had to make many such clandestine trips to different cities before Sonia was finally pregnant.

Sanjay and his family took it as God finally listening to their prayers. Only Sonia and Rahul knew the truth, which they would take to their graves.

The proud parents welcomed a chubby little girl at home.

After the birth, Rahul remained in contact with Sonia, more for his love for his daughter than anything else. Rahul and Sonia never even covertly referred to their secret.

***

Now, Rahul's daughter was in the house. It is so lovely to hear her say 'Pa.'

So, does this make Shilpa and Girish- brother-sister?

***

No, here is the bigger secret.

Sanjana, too, was unable to conceive. Medically, there was no problem with Rahul and Sanjana. She believed it was God's signal to them, telling them they would not have a child of their own. So, after completing the legal process, they adopted Girish from an orphanage in Goa. A full two years before Shilpa was born.

***

That is where similarities between the two families end.

Sanjay was proud of himself as he did not know the facts.

Sanjana was proud of herself because she knew everything, even about the birth of Shilpa. And it was she who wanted Shilpa as her daughter-in-law and ensured it happened.

Request, Please Don't Tell Girish Or Shilpa The Secret.

Acknowledgement

I must acknowledge the people who have contributed to making this book possible. I can openly name a few of them, and a few I can't. The people I can't understand why I can't name them. The people I name know their roles.

This book is dedicated to my mother, Smt Kanchan Lata Kotnala. She is the reason for whatever I have achieved in my life. And is dedicated to my wife Neha (Mamta) Kotnala, who is the source of all the encouragement I need.

I would also like to thank my in-laws, Late Shri Ved Prakash Kundlia and Late Smt Vijaya Kundlia. The sheer tingling of joy in their voice and pride in their eyes whenever a new book was published makes me work more and more. May they keep showering me with their blessings.

Above all, thanks to my father, Late Shri Ram Ballabh Kotnala, who blesses the family from heaven. I know that he would have been the person most happy with the release of these books, and I miss him the most.

Thanks are due to my kids, Prateek and Preetica, who may still wonder when and where these books take shape. Thank you for giving me the space and time to make this possible. And thanks to my dear Milo Kotnala, who was ever ready to remove the stress and play with me whenever there was writer's block.

Additionally, I am indebted to Ajay Lal who may have been the first read of the original draft many years back and who read the fresh draft and suggested all the changes. He also helped me pick the cover that you see.

About The Author

Sanjeev Kotnala, an IIM Ahmedabad alumnus.

He is a Brand and Marketing Advisor, Coach and Facilitator. In his blog titled **'Perceptions Adulterated with Reality'** **(www.sanjeevkotnala.com)**, he captures the experience and learning on the subject. He is proud of his weekly column 'KotMartial' published on www.mxmindia.com every Wednesday, for over 530 weeks, without a break.

Sanjeev already has Six books. **'Chimera Of Lansdowne'**- a novel with shades of paranormal. **'Life Reloaded'** and **'Reflections'**, an anthology of life impact stories. He also recently published his first book of poems- **'Always Questioning Life'**.

Pahaadi is an annual short story contest aimed to encourage talent in Uttarakhand and run by Sanjeev in memory of his father. Details can be accessed at **www.Sanjeevkotnala.com/Pahaadi.** This contest has resulted in three books of short stories curated by him. 2021- 'Pahaadi The Storytellers', 2022- 'The Runway

Suitcase and other stories'- and 2023- 'The Tiger in the Mountain and Other stories'.

Sanjeev is an avid doodler and treats it as meditation. He uses free doodling, mandala and Zen-tangle to do customised or conceptual doodles.

http://sanjeevkotnala.com/doodle-by-compulsive-doodler/

You can connect with Sanjeev Kotnala at **Twitter: s_kotnala** or mail at **www.intradia.in/contact**

Other Books By Sanjeev Kotnala

CHIMERA OF LANSDOWNE (Fiction)

The lives of five residents in the sleepy little town of Lansdowne in Uttarakhand are loosely connected. They have all been at the receiving end of independent unexplained experiences. Their past is intertwined with their present and maybe the future, in case it exists.

They can only beat the enemy collectively. However, they don't know the unseen and don't know who the Chimera of Lansdowne is.

Will they unite to take advantage of a once-in-a-lifetime opportunity? They have limited time on hand. Will they be able to connect the dots and find the key? Will they succeed in breaking the cycle that has started playing in their city?

***

Real Life Real Stories. The Impact stories.

Two books of Real-life Impact stories. Life reloaded – where 14 professionals shared their impact stories from personal and professional space. And Reflections, where the class of '87 of IIM Ahmedabad shared their stories.

PAHAADI- 1,2,3

Pahaadi is the short story contest for writers with roots in Uttarakhand run by Sanjeev Kotnala in memory f his father, the Late Shri Ram Ballabh Kotnala. The three books have selected stories curated by Sanjeev kotnala. Now in 2024- Pahaadi enters 4th season.

ALWAYS QUESTIONING LIFE.

A set of 21 poems that has Sanjeev Kotnala raising unanswered questions with his own perspective of expectations and experiences.

Blue Pencilled by Neena Bagga

Bagga, a Lady Shri Ram college graduate with a post-graduation in English from Delhi University, is an editor par excellence. As a freelance editor, she has edited many books and novels. She is a content editor for a couple of magazines.

She has blue-pencilled my first book,'Chimera Of Lansdowne', 'reflections' and the current novel you are reading, 'Enchanting Neeli.'

As an editor, she has checked the manuscript and read the drafts and contributed to providing inputs that have helped the whole construct of the novels and the anthology. However, I have made many changes from the last draft she approved, so if you find any error, you can partially blame it on me.

After three decades, she wears many hats: an educationist, a writer, an editor, and a dreamer with feet firmly planted.

About two decades back, Neena started 'Education Personified' coaching classes believing in customized education. She has contributed to the lives of thousands of children and young adults by enhancing their English Speaking and writing capabilities. She regularly conducts workshops on debating, elocution, creative writing, grammar, and vocabulary building for corporates, NGOs and other stakeholders. Last year, she taught more than 150 differently challenged youth and young adults to develop their English Language skills purely for employability.

The Song

Well, it is true that the song I have used in the book is one of my favourites and I don't know the exact lyrics by heart. I have used it the way I would sing.

I first heard this song in the majestic voice of my friend and batchmate at IIM Ahmedabad, Vinay Mahajan. This song then joined two other songs that are favourite. 'Humey Tunm Se Pyaar Kitna' from and film Kudrat - 'Mere Dil Mai Aaj Kya Hai' from film Daag.

I have publicly performed this song trice. Once at my marriage anniversary celebration at Lonawala before the family and friend. Then at IIM A batch reunion- where the comfort zone of only batchmates as an audience made me courageous enough to sing it- that too with Vinay Mahajan in audience. Similarly, I sung it in an event at Chennai last year. And I continue to sing it under the breath as I walk in the morning.

Here is the full song and apparently it is sung by late Akhlaq Ahmed- for a Pakistani film Bandish (1980) and the music was scored by late Robin Ghosh. It was picturised on Shabnam – Nadeem.

Sona Na Chandi, Na Koi Mehal Jaan-e-Mann
Tujh Ko Main, De Sakoongaa
Phir Bhi Yeh Waada Hai Tujh Se
Tu Jo Kare Pyar Mujh Se
Chota Sa Ghar Tujh Ko Doongaa
Dukh Sukh Ka Saathi Banoongaa
Sona Na Chandi, Na Koi Mehal Jaan-e-Mann
Tujh Ko Main, De Sakoongaa

Jab Shaam Ghar Laut Aaoongaa
Hansti Hui Tu Milaygee
Mit Jayen Gi Saari Sochein
Bahon Mein Jab Thaam Leygee
Chutti Ka Din Jab Hogaa
Hum Khoob Ghooma Karengey
Din Raat Honton Pe Apnay
Chahat Ke Naghmay Khileingey
Bechain Do Dil Milaingey
Sona Na Chandi, Na Koi Mehal Jaan-e-Mann
Tujh Ko Main, De Sakoongaa

Garmi Main Ja Kai Pahaaronpe
Ham Geet Gaaya Kareingey
Sardi Main Chup Ke Lihafon Mein
Kissay Sunaya Kareingey
Rut Ayay Gi Jab Baharon Ki
Phoolon Ki Maala Buneingey
Ja Kay Samandar Pe Dono
Seepon Se Moti Chuneingey
Lehron Ki Payal Suneingey

Sona Na Chandi, Na Koi Mehal Jaan-e-Mann
Tujh Ko Main, De Sakoongaa

Tankhaa Main Jab Le Kay Aaoongaa
Haathon Main Teray Hi Doongaa
Jab Kharch Hon Ge Woh Paisay
Main Tujh Se Jhagraa Karoongaa
Phir Aisa Hoga Tu Mujh Se
Kuch Dair Roothi Rahaygi
Sochay Gi Jab Apnay Dil Main
Tu Muskura Kai Barhay Gi
Aa Ker Galay Se Lagaygi...

Sona Na Chandi, Na Koi Mehal Jaan-e-Mann
Tujh Ko Main, De Sakoon Ga
Sona Na Chandi, Na Koi Mehal Jaan-e-Mann
Tujh Ko Main, De Sakoon Ga

www.ingramcontent.com/pod-product-compliance
Lightning Source LLC
Chambersburg PA
CBHW051247250726
48656CB00004B/1163